Vinegar Pie

and Other Tales
of the
Grand Traverse Region

Vinegar Pie
and Other Tales

of the
Grand Traverse Region

Special Millenium 2000 Edition

HORIZON BOOKS   TRAVERSE CITY, MI

LIBRARY OF CONGRESS CATALOG CARD NUMBER 58-12684
ISBN 0-915937-00-X (HC)
ISBN 0-915937-06-9 (PB)

PUBLISHED BY

HORIZON BOOKS, 243 E. FRONT ST., TRAVERSE CITY, MI 49684

to Alice, My Wife, and

to Jay P. Smith

Forword

MOST HISTORIANS AGREE that it takes at least a hundred years for any community—hamlet, town, city—to acquire a history. That's because it takes that long for its people to get the necessary perspective. Until then they are much more interested in the present and the future than in the past.

So perhaps it was no accident that the fascinating stories of Al Barnes began to appear regularly in the home-town newspaper, the Traverse City *Record-Eagle*, in the middle 1940s, just about one hundred years after the city's birth. "Vinegar Pie", a collection of stories about Traverse City and the Grand Traverse Region, was the first important historical work on the area since the publication of Dr. M.L. Leach's "History of the Grand Traverse Region" in 1884.

Al was fortunate to have the *Record-Eagle's* great editor, Jay P. Smith, to aid and encourage him. Smith was a native of Traverse City. He was familiar with the old Traverse City tales, knew where all the bodies were buried, and was himself a lover of local history and a nifty writer, too.

Al was also fortunate in being able to interview personally so many of the area's old-timers who had helped make that history. He was a pioneer in this field. It was he who first discovered Traverse City's rich historical heritage of colorful people and events.

They're all here in "Vinegar Pie", surging back to life in its pages: Police Chief

John "Blackjack" Rennie and his black horse Dogwood; an Indian uprising that almost happened; Widow McGinnis and her long sleep; Charlie Augustine and his bamboo airplane; "Father" of Traverse City Perry Hannah competing with local lumberjacks in log rolling contests in town on the Boardman River on Independence Days; Eric the Swede, who disappeared without collecting his back wages; Flip Gillespie, the fastest draw in rough-and-tumble Walton Junction; Chief William Jake and the Indian Settlement; Wexford, the ghost of a ghost town—the list goes on and on.

Harry A. "Al" Barnes was born in Madison, South Dakota. He wrote his first published piece, a crop report for a farming magazine, at the age of 13. He quit school in the ninth grade, but his life-long self-education included Latin and algebra. He worked at various jobs-musician, truck driver, and free-lance writer-before joining the *Record-Eagle* news staff in 1937 at the age of 32.

Barnes was an all-around newspaper man. A self-taught photographer and photoengraver, he specialized in feature stories with an historical angle. He published four books, "One Hundred Years from the Old Mission", "Vinegar Pie", "Supper in the Evening", and "Let's Fly Backward!". He died on December 12, 1995.

Larry Wakefield
Writer/Historian
Traverse City, Michigan
25 March 2000

Preface

THE MAJORITY of the following stories first appeared under my by-line in the *Traverse City Record-Eagle*. They were written under the stress and strain of a daily deadline with its inevitable consequences. Accordingly, some of them had to be revised for publication in book form. However, most of them are presented in their original form with only minor alterations.

Credit to the scores of people who assisted in the preparation of this book is impossible. Its compilation covers a span of ten years, and many of the pioneers who were so helpful have passed on. I am humble in my acknowledgment of the priceless help given me by all of them. Documentation, research, and long hours of study have combined to lend great accuracy to the manuscript. Of course, the old files of the *Grand Traverse Herald*, the *Morning Record* and the *Record-Eagle* contributed much to the effort. Their availability, through the co-operation of the publisher, A. C. Batdorff, was, indeed, a favor without price.

My appreciation, which I find difficult to express properly, goes to Dr. Harold Basilius, director of Wayne State University Press and his editorial staff. Their assistance, and their kind understanding of my problems and short-comings, especially during the final editing, have added greatly to the value of the book.

I especially thank Jay P. Smith, one of the editors on the *Traverse City Record-Eagle*, without whose great knowledge of pioneers and pioneer happenings in the Grand Traverse region, this book could not have been presented. Its authenticity, its color and readability are due, in a great measure, to his assistance and criticism. To him and to all others who have helped, I say in Chippewa: Weweni ganawendamog ki debweiendamowiniwa (Keep well your faith).

Al Barnes
TRAVERSE CITY, MICHIGAN
May 14, 1958

Introduction

WITH THE OPENING of the bridge across the Straits of Mackinac, more and more, people are making their first visit to the northern part of the Lower Peninsula of Michigan enroute to see, and to cross, the bridge to the Upper Peninsula of Michigan. In traveling over the highways in this part of the State, they pass beautiful lakes and through scenic forests, rounding curves with new vistas at each turn, with here and there large clumps of white birch set against the shimmering waters of inland lakes. The view through the leaves and branches of the trees is matchless in beauty, particularly in that part of the northlands of the Lower Peninsula known as the Grand Traverse area. With this awareness of the region's regal beauty comes a longing to know more about the country itself. Question after question comes to mind. What was it like a hundred or more years ago? Who were the inhabitants and early settlers? What of the Indians? While Lincoln and Douglas were debating in Illinois, what was happening in the great State of Michigan just south and north of 45° latitude?

The countryside is filled with surprises for the traveler. Think of a fine bookstore tucked away near the shoreline of Grand Traverse Bay with an excellent selection of the modern and the old, and a discriminating proprietor in charge; or the sight of a large flock of white swans sailing on the same bay with all the dignity of an Admiral's fleet passing in review; or a century old church or mission, still in good condition and still ministering to Indians and settlers alike; or the post office location where the first postmistress in Michigan carried on her duties. If we move from landscape to seascape, we find the indentation of the waters of the Great Lakes surrounding us, making up the longest shoreline of any state in the Union. Along this shoreline and along the edges of the picturesque inland lakes, we find the matchless beauty of the maple, the oak, the birch, the elm, the pine and the evergreen. They are beautiful at all seasons of the year. In fact, nature in the Grand Traverse country is a strong exponent of the four seasons, and each one of them can be delightful.

If events have a way of shaping things to come, then we can readily come to the conclusion that the timber owners and the lumberjacks were but clearing the way for a new type of civilization and culture.

But they didn't know about it then or afterward. The second growth of timber has covered the scars left by the removal of the original stands, but the beauty of the countryside lingers on even more beautiful and stimulating, and what is more to the point, it has not yet been spoiled or desecrated by unsightly structures. In such a setting and on some of the sites formerly lumber camps, we find today educational institutions of meritorious and transcendent value, summer camps for boys and girls, institutions like the National Music Camp at Interlochen, the Leelanau Schools, Northwestern Michigan College, Shady Trails Camp for speech correction, all organized by dedicated people.

It is proper to add that there are many well-known writers and artists who have taken up permanent residence in this unparalleled and invigorating Grand Traverse region, and it is fast becoming a center of culture.

Al Barnes, the author of this book, makes the area live as it was in the past, as he records the events of upwards of a hundred years ago or more. He writes about the activities carried on in the newly established settlements of Northwest Michigan—stories of logging and sawmills, and woodworking plants making woodenware, butter dishes, chopping bowls, clothespins, furniture, cooper products, barrels and boxes, poles and ties, flour and grist mills, woolen mills, brick and cement plants, and many other commercial and manufacturing activities. He weaves in a bit of folklore, too.

Each chapter of *Vinegar Pie and Other Tales* is a story in itself, yet there is a continuity tying all the chapters together. You can pick up the book, read a section or two, put it down and pick it up again later and never lose the main theme. It is an ideal travel or bedside book for those who like to read before turning out the light at night. In addition to delightful reading, it will give you plenty to think about, too. One of the best examples of gerrymandering is the story of the removal of the county seat of Wexford County from the village of Sherman, thence to the village of Manton, and finally to Clam Lake, now Cadillac. Read about it, you will enjoy the politics and the intrigue. The author has recorded many historical facts and events, important in the history of Michigan, that will keep the Michigan Historical Commission busy in the years ahead marking places deserving recognition. Many others might well be marked by local or county historical societies.

To those of you who have not heard the story of the passing of the passenger pigeon from the lips of your grandparents or great grandparents, the author has written a vivid description of the migrations of these fine birds and their final demise. To those of you who are interested in sailing vessels, and lake craft of all kinds, you have a treat in store as you read about the storm tossed ships lost on the Great Lakes, and on some of the other large inland lakes. If it is Indians: Did you know that there was at one time in Michigan a little band of Ottawa Indians who were "unbelievers," who did not believe in the Great Spirit? You can read about Sitting Bull and the emissaries he sent to gain support of local tribes for a general Indian uprising.

No more need be said. Mr. Barnes has rendered a great service to his community and to his State and to the descendents of the people who took part in the events he describes. He has made a record which should be real source material for genealogical researchers.

St. Augustine in his *Confessions* said, "men go abroad to wonder at the heights of mountains, the lofty billows of the sea, the long courses of the rivers, the vast compass of the ocean, and the circular motions of the stars." We agree, but we would urge that the northlands of Michigan also abound in unforgettable beauty, with a history of events that match and inspire the best found anywhere, all brought into true perspective by Mr. Barnes.

Roscoe O. Bonisteel
MEMBER, BOARD OF GOVERNORS, WAYNE STATE UNIVERSITY
MEMBER, BOARD OF REGENTS, UNIVERSITY OF MICHIGAN

Contents

ILLUSTRATIONS

Traverse City, 1865—just a row of frame buildings on the Boardman River.

The Union Street Bridge in Traverse City, 1865. Today it is in the very heart of the downtown area. The view is to the south.

Said Martin Newstead, pioneer lumberjack:

Vinegar pie? Hell, yes! Better than any fancy cookin' you ever et. Ain't no lumberjack what didn't eat vinegar pie. And prune pie and dried apple pie and salt sidemeat and sour-dough pancakes. Hell, yes!

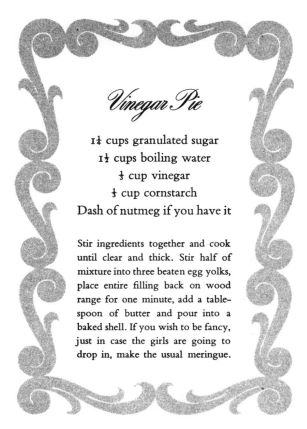

Vinegar Pie

1¼ cups granulated sugar
1¼ cups boiling water
¼ cup vinegar
¼ cup cornstarch
Dash of nutmeg if you have it

Stir ingredients together and cook until clear and thick. Stir half of mixture into three beaten egg yolks, place entire filling back on wood range for one minute, add a tablespoon of butter and pour into a baked shell. If you wish to be fancy, just in case the girls are going to drop in, make the usual meringue.

Traverse City, 1958. The pier in the left foreground was once the location of the Hannah, Lay and Company sawmill and the hub of northern Great Lakes shipping.

THE
BUSTLING
CITY

. . . there was a procession of Indians down Union Street. There was Chief Ahgosa and Chief Petoskey . . . flaunting eagle-feather war bonnets . . . . Bringing up the rear of the procession, which caused housewives to hide their children and bolt their doors, came two tall braves wearing eagle feathers in their hair. They were couriers from the encampment of Sitting Bull . . . . there was a scare . . . . in the Bert Wilhelm home all the guns were loaded . . . .

An Historical Note

In 1851, Perry Hannah came to the Grand Traverse region to open a new frontier and build what was later to be a giant empire in the business world. The story of his arrival, in his own words, was written in 1899 and printed in a souvenir edition of the Sunday edition of the *Morning Record*, a newspaper published in Traverse City.

"THE YOUNG of today look to the early pioneer settler as one who had to endure great privation and experience untold hardships. This was not true with the first people of Grand Traverse. I never saw a happier or a more contented crowd than were the pioneers of Traverse City. It seemed to me that they must all have taken lessons of John Stuart Mill, who said that he had learned to seek his happiness by limiting his desires rather than attempting to satisfy them. I never spent more pleasant hours in my life than I did with the dozen or two that made up our entire number the first year.

"Last winter, Mr. Vanderbilt was asked what he would choose for a Christmas present. His reply was, 'Give me an appetite.' It could not be furnished. Wealth could not buy it. No one ever complained in the early days in Traverse City of suffering from such a complaint. We were all happier than was the millionaire.

"In the first days of May, 1851, I left Chicago on the little schooner *Venus* in company with Captain Harry Boardman, a rich old farmer who lived in DuPage County, about five miles southeast of Naperville. The captain, two years before, had furnished his son, Horace, with money to plant a mill on the little creek in the western part of our town, but experience had taught him that it would take more than the avails of one Illinois farm to sustain an operating mill with the present prices of lumber, hence he gave our firm an option for the sale of the mill and his landed estate, that is now Traverse City.

"Captain Peter Nelson, one of the finest old Dane sailors who ever walked on the deck of a ship, was master of the little schooner *Venus* and who will be known to many of our present settlers as manager of the lighthouse at Northport, of later years.

"We had left Chicago on our journey to the north but two or three days, when we met one of those terrible northeast gales, which were always sure to last a full three days. We were well down Lake Michigan, and our brave old seaman decided that we must weather out the storm instead of returning, and never a more terrific time did I see in my life than those three days, pounding backward and forward across Lake Michigan. As soon as the gale subsided, we wended our way along into Grand Traverse Bay, on one of the pleasantest, most beautiful and charming evenings that was ever seen; we rounded into the Old Mission harbor, just as the sun was going down behind the tops of the tall maples that stood on the ridge in the center of the peninsula. It was one of those serene and beautiful evenings, with the southerly breeze not more than half a mile per hour—as we entered the harbor—and on the banks of the western side sat perhaps forty or fifty old Indian hunters. I could see with my glass that each one had his pipe in his mouth, and they were sitting on the bank watching the movement of our ship, chatting and talking, as happy as one ever could imagine. To the rear of them were perhaps forty or fifty nice whitewashed wigwams, and around them could be seen the Indian women doing the drudgery of the night, and the Indian children hallooing here and there in their evening skips of play. Further up, in among the tall maples, could be seen the large white mansion of Rev. Peter Dougherty. Further up beyond that, the Indian ponies, with their bells on their necks—their fore feet shackled together—were jumping from place to place, looking for the last meal for the night. Still further up were the great tall maples down behind which the sun was disappearing. I said to myself as I looked upon that beautiful scene that if 'ignorance is bliss, it is folly to be wise,' for a more beautiful picture I never saw in my life.

"After landing a few traps that we had brought for Mr. Dougherty, we wended our way around the turn; and as Captain Nelson was nearly worn out, he laid himself down a blanket by the wheelman, ordering him to keep straight down the bay until he was well past the Mission point, and then call him.

"In a moment's time, the old captain, tired out as he was, was well along the

3

'land of nod,' and the good-hearted sailor, seeing how nicely he was sleeping, thought it cruel to waken him and he could steer the ship around into West Bay without any difficulty. In a few moments, thump, thump, thump, went the little ship over the rocks. In a moment's time the old captain was on his feet, and then, I tell you, all was blue! We had run over a ledge of rocks into a pond, where there was plenty of water, and how to get out was the great sequel. After using the leadline and sounding all around, the captain determined that the ship must be hauled back exactly in the same place that it went in, hence all hands had to work. The anchors were carried out in the small boats, and with the aid of a little extra south wind that had raised the water, we were able to get our boat back into its proper position, just as the sun was coming over the great green maples between Torch Lake and the bay.

"We soon made our way up to the mill. There we met the captain's son, but all hands were taking a little rest. As there had been a shower an hour before, the boys couldn't work outdoors, the good natured son had stopped the mill, allowing all hands to go in and have a game of euchre. This made the old captain—Harry Boardman—more willing than ever to sell, as he was fully satisfied that there was not quite push enough in his son, Horace, to make a successful lumberman.

"The next move was to prepare the packs for a trip up the Boardman (which we named after old Captain Harry) to ascertain if there was lumber sufficient on its banks to afford to locate a larger mill at the mouth of the Boardman. We journeyed up on the west and south side of the river to a point about where Mayfield now stands, crossing over to Hog's Back Lake, and thence down again—making up our minds that we had seen fifty millions of timber. Since that time, over four hundred millions have been cut and brought down the Boardman. Thus commences the beginning of the earliest days of Traverse City, and today we number ten thousand inhabitants.

"I have been often asked if I am not surprised at the great change which has taken place in these forty years. I can only answer that my expectations have not been realized. I looked forward within ten years to see a town here of twenty thousand inhabitants. I had seen cities grow up on the western prairies in less time, of greater size; but I did not take into consideration that great maples and elms . . . covered our county, and that it would take time to clear them away.

4

It was considered in those days a great task to get rid of them, never expecting to see them worth what they are today. Yet I do believe that we will see the time when Traverse City will reach its twenty thousand inhabitants; and I shall stay a little time longer, seating myself in an easy chair, in the afternoon of my life—watching Traverse City grow, believing that it will be one of the most beautiful towns in the state of Michigan."

An Indian Uprising—Almost!

HISTORIANS have always referred to the Traverse City community as a peaceful area where war, even a threat of war, has never been known.

How wrong they are.

Traverse City once knew the fear of war and saw its shadow passing kitchen windows, witnessed its prediction in the smoke of pitch pine fires and brilliant war bonnets of Indian chieftains.

It happened a long time ago, to be sure, and no one bothered at the time to record the facts or make note of the seriousness of the situation. Only pioneer memories have made this record possible.

Union Street was known as Sawdust Road because it was paved with sawdust from Bay Street to what is now Sixteenth Street. Along the road there were only a few homes and buildings.

On the west side of the road, between Seventh and Tenth, there were the Furtsch store, Bartak's, Wilhelm's, the Louis Miller home, Charley Dupre's, and the homes of the Lees, Holdsworths and Bakers; on the east side of the road were Boardman House, Chaloupka's saloon, the Kyselka home, the St. Francis convent, Mattison's drug store and the Sabin, Weidenhanner and Dezorme homes.

At this time Sitting Bull was on the warpath in the West and on June 25, 1876, had wiped out General George Armstrong Custer and his men at the Little Big Horn in Montana.

Sitting Bull was a brilliant man and did not overlook the possibility of stirring up unrest among all the tribes of the nation. His scouts visited whenever there was a concentration of Indians.

Traverse City was no exception.

6

On a warm June morning there was a stir among the local Indian population. They had decided to have a council of war. One local chief not mentioned in many records, Chief Peewash, lived on the banks of Boot Lake, just south of Traverse City. In his ancient home on Fernwood Hill it was decided to call all the leaders of the local tribes to decide whether or not the white men should be pushed from the region.

Thus it was that Boot Lake, until recently a part of the Country Club golf course, became the site of a powwow which was to decide the history of the Grand Traverse region for generations to come.

During the early morning of that day there was a procession of Indians down Sawdust Road.

There was Chief Ahgosa and Chief Petoskey, wearing their tribal costumes and flaunting eagle-feather war bonnets. Close behind them came a number of braves from local settlements. Then came Chief Blackbird, wearing the jet-black wing of a raven in his hair, and Chief Redbird with brilliant red feathers.

From High Island (the Beaver Islands) came John Cornstalk and his men, from Kewadin came John Gingway and his following. Joe Greenleaf came with a delegation from Cross Village.

Bringing up the rear of the procession, which caused housewives to hide their children and bolt their doors, came two tall braves wearing eagle feathers in their hair. They were couriers from the encampment of Sitting Bull.

Also attending the meeting was Father Mrack, a missionary to the Indians along Lake Michigan. The good priest had established a mission at Eagletown (now Peshabestown) in Leelanau County and was a powerful influence among the tribes.

All day long there was a cloud of smoke over the encampment at Boot Lake. Council fires burned and smoldered. The delegates talked on.

Toward evening the procession returned down Sawdust Road, and still later came the couriers from the camp of Sitting Bull. They had failed.

It was later learned that Father Mrack had been the deciding influence. His persuasive speech and his knowledge of the Indians and their ways had avoided war.

But there was a scare. For example, in the Bert Wilhelm home all the guns were loaded and knives and meat cleavers were placed handy; the doors were

7

locked, and a tame bear, which the family had for a pet, was turned loose in the kitchen.

That was the only war scare ever to hit the Traverse City community. One local native, Indian Jake, who lived in a slab wigwam just north of the public library, attended the session but there is no record that he ever discussed what transpired.

Descendants of these early Indian leaders still live at Cross Village, at Petoskey, and in Traverse City. They are like any other citizens, and one would never guess, to visit them, that their ancestors once discussed the possibility of war against the Traverse City region.

"Squaw Point" at the mouth of the Boardman River, about 1880. This was a favorite gathering place of the Ottawa and Chippewa Indians. They met here in the fall to hunt and pick berries inland.

The "Widder's" Lost Weekend

WIDOW McGINNIS had a lost week-
end. Not in the contemporary manner, however. The widow Jane McGinnis
slept through a whole weekend — thirty-six straight hours.

"Widder" McGinnis, as she was called by her many friends in the early days,
lived on the outskirts of Traverse City in Slabtown, sometimes waggishly called
Bagdad. It was a collection of shanties and small houses west of the big mill,
most of which had been constructed from slabs, edgings and odds and ends of
lumber from scrap piles.

Mrs. McGinnis was an angular person with warm gray eyes. Her face was
slightly marked from a session with smallpox in her youth. Widowed early, she
had one son, Jock. Her income came from her services as a nurse to the residents
of the lumbering town of Traverse City, and her sole companion, when Jock
was out in the woods, was a cat, a big yellow one, she called Oliver. Wherever
Mrs. McGinnis went, Oliver went also. Sometimes she carried the animal in a
shopping basket with a cover over it.

At home in her Slabtown shack, the "widder" would knit, smoke her pipe,
and relax as much as her restless Scotch nature would permit. Come nighttime,
she would retire early. "The days are so short," she would remark, "and karasene
thirty cents a gallon."

Her broad brogue was typically Scotch.

As near as can be determined today, the McGinnis shack was located just
west of Rickerd's Monument Works, probably on ground now traversed by
Grandview Parkway. There was one window which looked out over the bay
and a door facing the east. An old wood range provided the heat and cooking
facilities. Mention is made in old copies of the *Traverse City Morning Record* that

9

Mrs. McGinnis had a fine view of "the bight of the bay" from her window. It was the day before Christmas in the early eighties. There is no record of the exact date. A wintry wind was howling off the bay and the thermometer was dropping rapidly. Christmas day was scheduled to be a white one and cold. Jock McGinnis was out with a gang in the woods, and the widow was whiling away her time knitting a pair of double-yarn mittens for him. She expected him home for the holiday. Now and again she would glance out of the north window of the shanty and calculate the temperature. Time after time she would poke the fire and sometimes add another chunk of wood.

She finished the mittens and approved their wooly cuffs, meditating, as she related later, that when Jock came home on the "morrow" she would have him take them to Patrick's Shoe Shop and get them faced for better wear.

For supper she fried two slices of salt pork, sliced some boiled potatoes in a sizzling iron skillet and brewed a cup of hot coffee. Oliver got one of the slices of pork.

After supper, Mrs. McGinnis donned a linsey-woolsey "sack" over her yellow flannel bed gown, wrapped a shawl about her shoulders and retired.

The wind got worse. Heavy snow swirled out of the northwest and huge drifts all but hid Slabtown.

Christmas day dawned cold and blustery. Parties which had been scheduled were postponed and the village dug in for a cold snap. All that could be seen of the Widder McGinnis' shack was the rusted chimney. It was completely buried under a giant snow drift.

First note of her plight came when Patrick, the shoemaker, mentioned, in a conversation with John Norris, that it was fortunate the widow was away. "She's over to the boarding house," he explained, "been there a week. Somebody sick over there."

Christmas day passed and, on the day after, Patrick noticed smoke coming from the chimney. It was then that the neighbors got together and began digging through the drift.

Mrs. Jane McGinnis was fine. She was all rested. In the drift-darkened shanty she had slept through two nights and a day.

Informed that she had lost Christmas day, she refused to believe it. A coachman from the Perry Hannah residence arrived with gifts of clothing, belated because of the storm, and a Christmas dinner. Mrs. Hannah had sent a fresh apple pie.

Telling the story later, Mrs. McGinnis saw little humor in the incident.

"I was that taken aback," she said, "that a child could have knocked me over easy. And when them menfolks came a-knockin' at my door I was clean vexed with them for disturbin' a lady in the middle of the night.

"It's a fine mon is Mr. Patrick. I'd be glad for his foin leddy wife to know my opinion of him . . . and she too proud to live with him because forsooth, he takes a wee drap too much now and then."

The widow died on December 26, 1891 and was buried in Oakwood Cemetery, Traverse City. The day of her death was the anniversary of her lost weekend.

Jock, her son, eventually moved away, probably following the timber.

Interior of the S.E. Wait Drugstore, Traverse City, 1885. It was the first drugstore in Traverse City. Mr. Wait is pictured in the center. In the foreground is Frank Parker, an assistant. The other men are unknown.

Panic in Traverse City

TRAVERSE CITY was in an uproar. It was the spring of 1905 and Front Street was beginning to take on the look of a metropolis. There were forty-eight factories in the city, and a survey showed that 1,367 men were employed in them. Stores were well stocked with the latest of everything.

All of this was in danger of being lost by flood. That was the cause of the uproar. Housewives lived in dread of an avalanche of water which might come roaring down from Boardman Valley at any moment and which would surely wipe out the bustling city.

Word had reached town that a young fellow named Waldo Culver was going to drain Arbutus Lake, ten miles south, into Boardman Valley. If he drained Arbutus, the lake's lower level would in turn bring Spider Lake level down, because Spider Lake was forty-seven feet above Arbutus. Moreover, between Spider and Arbutus Lake, was another lake, Spring, which would add to the flood waters.

With each telling the story got bigger and more weird. Young Culver was a chap (according to rumors) with a grudge against civilization and he wanted to wipe out the city. He wanted to drain the lakes to utilize the fertile bottom lands. All sorts of tales flew thick and fast.

Jack Rennie, chief of police in Traverse City at that time, was approached and asked to investigate.

Early one morning Chief Rennie harnessed his black horse, Dogwood, to his buggy and headed for the lakes.

There was activity all right. Rennie found a mite of a man in a wide-brimmed hat busy running a stream of water from Spring Lake to Arbutus. He was doing a mighty big job—all alone.

Rennie spent some time visiting and going over the project before returning to Traverse City to await the flood. Everything young Culver was doing was entirely within the law.

The background of the project, according to Culver, was as follows:

It seems that two brothers, Ray and Will Jackson, who lived in the Mayfield community, decided that there should be a lot of easy money in the cranberry business. There was certainly no need to import berries from the East when there was a perfect opportunity to raise them in the Grand Traverse region. All that needed to be done was to fill a marsh area between Arbutus and Spider Lakes, bringing the land a little closer to the surface to allow the cranberry plants to grow.

With this in mind, they secured government water-level statistics, got a permit from the state of Michigan to tap the waters of Spider, and hired young Culver to begin the job.

It started in the spring of 1905. Culver hired a team of horses and threw up an earth dam at the west end of Spring Lake. From this point he started to dig a ditch through the woods to Arbutus Lake. It would be a job to stagger a man today. He had only his brawn, an axe, shovel, and a dogged determination.

"Jail Hill" in Traverse City, 1896, during the William Jennings Bryan and William McKinley presidential campaign.

13

Culver's purpose was to run the stream along a high sand bank, cut it away with a sluice stream and wash the sand into the bottom land. The ditch was completed during the summer of 1905 and the sand-washing operations got under way.

Slowly the bank was cut back and the sand flowed into the proposed cranberry marsh. As the bank receded, the bed of the ditch was moved over to give it a new "bite." Culver said he firmly believed that this work was the first sand pumping operation ever made.

With the work well under way, the operation was suspended for the winter. It was started again after spring breakup in 1906. In the summer following, the excitement really ran high. The constant drain of water from Spring and Spider lakes was making its mark on Arbutus. The water level began to climb and, by midsummer, the overflow began crossing the sand trail at the junction of what is now Hobbs Highway and Arbutus Road. That was the only time there was any danger of Arbutus Lake running into Boardman River and then into Traverse City.

The sand pumping operation continued until June, 1908, when the Jacksons lost interest. The work was then abandoned. The marks are still there. The sand which was pumped into the flats is now pasture. The High Lake Trail, which is a new road, crosses directly over the spot. The old ditch which sluiced the water from Spring and Spider Lakes is still as much in evidence as it was when young Culver first dug it. The sand bank with its tumbled pine stumps is a scar that can still be seen from the trail, and the three "locks" at Spider, though long since gone, have left their mark.

The pipe which carried the sand wash from the bank, sixty-five rods of it, twelve inches in diameter, has long since rusted away.

The panic is only a memory.

14

The Oval Wood Dish

ONLY IN collections, in an occasional antique shop, and in museums, can one find an example of the work once created in Traverse City by the Oval Wood Dish Company.

Once a giant in northern Michigan industrial circles, the O.W.D. was a child of the hardwood forests. From clear blocks of maple, beech, oak, and birch, the company manufactured butter dishes, chopping bowls, clothespins, and, in later years, veneer lard containers which have long since been replaced by fiber and paper containers.

The Oval Wood Dish Company was started in Mancelona in 1883 and came to Traverse City in April 1892, when the first ground was broken on the banks of Boardman Lake near the Chesapeake and Ohio Railway Depot.

To say the O.W.D. was a giant in industry is putting the facts mildly. It was the largest company of its kind in the world and, for a period of twenty-six years, was the backbone of the Traverse City industrial machine.

The sawmill, which provided squared wood bolts for the factory, was started in December 1892 and, during the time it operated here, cut for manufacture into merchandise over twenty-one million feet of hardwood. Each year saw a thousand railroad cars stacked with dishes and clothespins for the markets of the world. One year, shipment even reached a total of twelve hundred cars.

Wintertime employment reached as high as five hundred men and women, and during the summer months it dropped to three hundred and fifty or four hundred persons. The payroll in Traverse City averaged $200,000 annually. In that day, a half century ago, a payroll of this magnitude was certainly one to be coveted by surrounding communities.

Several factories and mills in the region utilized the heavy hardwood stands inland. There was a factory at Walton Junction which produced lasts for shoemakers; a plant at Beitner which produced knock-down furniture; a handle mill in Traverse City in addition to a number of other mills which produced hardwood lumber of high quality. Not a single factory, however, ever reached the financial and production status of the O.W.D.

Then came a crisis in the life of the concern. The virgin stands of hardwood moved farther and farther inland. Logging operations became more remote and the transportation of the logs became more and more of a problem. For the production of the thin wooden dishes which had become so popular, it was necessary to secure only top quality logs and these were becoming increasingly scarce.

In 1916, it was decided that the industry must move. A survey of eastern

The Oval Wood Dish Company, Traverse City, around the turn of the century. It manufactured a wide variety of wooden dishes, clothespins, baskets and other wood items. When the timber became depleted, the plant was moved to New York state, where it is still in operation.

United States showed that the area around Tupper Lake, New York, was most ideally fitted to the future needs of the company. The area had a seemingly limitless supply of timber and the country was not unlike the Grand Traverse region where the O.W.D. had prospered.

The decision to move to New York was a momentous one locally. It meant that a great source of revenue for the community would be lost. Many families, choosing to move with the organization, were scheduled to be uprooted and to settle in a strange community. Nearly a hundred persons decided to make the move. Of those who went to Tupper Lake with the O.W.D., only two are still living. They are Gerald Hull, grandson of H. S. Hull, one of the founders of the company, and Charles Foote.

An institution such as Oval Wood Dish, with an established market, and more than an average amount of foresight, does not die overnight.

Today, at Tupper Lake, the firm is still operating and filling a place in the economy of its Franklin County home. It is the largest single industry there.

Forest management is maintaining a steady flow of raw materials from its 40,000 acres of timbered holdings.

Only its manufactured items are changing as the modern age requires. Instead of wooden salad and butter bowls and wire-end dishes, the concern turns out millions of little wooden sticks for ice cream bars, wooden spoons for take-out foods and picnics, wooden forks and small flat spoons. In dime stores, grocery stores, and others, all over the nation the trade names of "Ritespoon" and "Ritefork" are well known.

And today, as a half century ago, the O.W.D. leaders and executives are constantly exploring new fields in an effort to maintain the leadership of a company which was first established in the little lumbering town of Mancelona in 1883 and which left Traverse City in 1918 for a more plentiful source of raw materials.

Locally, the industry was a casualty of the wanton lumbering policy of the day. It was thought that the timber of the region would never become depleted. Forest management was unheard of and the selective cutting now practiced by lumbermen was only a dream.

Locally, there are hundreds of folks who still remember the chime whistle of Oval Wood Dish. They remember the long trains carrying wooden dishes to the nation. Too, they remember the payroll and its contribution to the regional economy.

There isn't a single sign today to show that the company ever operated here. The big drying sheds were taken apart and shipped west where they were rebuilt into sheep barns. Thirteen carloads of material were transferred for the purpose.

An aftermath of the existence of the factory was the deadhead timber left in the bottom of Boardman Lake. Early estimates indicated that between three and four million board feet of hardwood logs were on the bottom. A portable mill was set up under the direction of Charles Longnecker but no records are available of the amount of timber that was salvaged.

Still the largest factory of its kind in the world, the O.W.D. now has subsidiary organizations also producing wood items. It maintains its own airport. In the actual manufacture of wooden spoons, it has a payroll of five hundred; in addition, approximately one hundred and fifty men are engaged in the lumbering end of the industry. There are sixty acres of ground to house the activities of the concern, exclusive of its timbered holdings. Approximately three hundred and fifty thousand feet of floor space are covered for actual manufacturing operations.

So, as a tearful ballad, written in Traverse City in 1918 and entitled, "The Passing of O.W.D.," so appropriately predicted, the O.W.D. will never die.

Remember the Glidden?

THE GLIDDEN truck, with its cast grill radiator and hard-rubber tires, was made in Traverse City, and there aren't a half dozen men left who remember it.

In fact, there were very few people who ever did see the Glidden—even in transit, since they were assembled, painted, tested and crated in a watertight container for foreign shipment right in the factory.

It was the Glidden truck which ended the era of the automobile making in Traverse City when its manufacturer, the Napoleon Motors Company, floundered in a sea of financial uncertainty to finally sink under the pressure of creditors and disorganization.

Many people remember the Napoleon motor car and the Napoleon truck. It was made in the building now (1958) occupied by the Traverse City Garage.

Many people in northern Michigan would rather forget the fling they had at speculating in Napoleon Motors stock, because the pretty green and white stock certificates, issued in denominations of $10.00, came to a day when they weren't worth more than the paper they were printed on. One stockholder, having acquired a lot of stock in lieu of wages while he was employed by the firm, had enough to paper the inside of his "little building" at his fishing camp.

The story of Napoleon vehicles was one of misadventure for many community residents. At the time, 1918, it looked like a real chance to get in on the ground floor of the automotive industry.

The Ross automobile, manufactured in Napoleon, Ohio, had encountered financial difficulties and was looking for new and greener pastures. After a series of meetings with local business leaders, the firm felt that a sale of capital stock to the amount of $150,000 would start a plant in production in Traverse City.

Start they did, but without sufficient money to continue the industry. Since only a little over $100,000 of the stock had been sold, another series of drives and campaigns was necessary. On January 5, 1918, a meeting was called at the Chamber of Commerce to discuss the precarious financial position of the concern, and E. D. Misner, general manager of the plant, stated that with proper backing he could produce two automobiles a day. It was decided to engage Theodore Kerkhoff to conduct a drive to dispose of the balance of the stock, which amounted to $44,300.

The first few days of the sale brought an astounding fact to light. The "big men," as Kerkhoff called them, were leaving the stock alone while the laborers of the city were stepping up to purchase one, two, or three, of the $10.00 certificates.

World War I was on and there were restrictions of fuel, shortage of materials, Liberty bond drives, and a score of other distractions.

Publicity released on the sale of the balance of the stock was conflicting. Kerkhoff released a story that the stock would be taken by the "big interests" unless local people came to the rescue. He said he wanted to give the Traverse City folks an opportunity to "get in on the ground floor" and was, therefore, withholding the sale from the industrial moguls.

On February 7, 1918, company officials announced that over half of the remaining stock had been sold. A later statement, made by Frank Trude, then secretary-treasurer of the concern, stated that only $10,000 of the stock had been bought, a direct contradiction of the earlier stories released by the Kerkhoff sales force.

About this time Kerkhoff admitted his sales program had been a failure, the company was tottering, and the city of Cadillac held a big public meeting for the purpose of attracting the industry. Cadillac citizens sent an investigating committee to Traverse City to study the plant. Their concensus was "but for the fact that the plant is located in Traverse City, it would succeed."

In an effort to save the business, a call was placed to C. R. Hardy, Louisville, Ky. He had a reputation as a "doctor of sick industry." He reviewed the situation and said that he could cure the illness in two weeks if he could establish a $30,000 trust fund with the Chamber of Commerce as operating capital. Another meeting was called and enthusiasm resulted in the raising of all but $5,000 of the amount called for. The sale of the trust fund certificates made a list that resembled a directory of local business leaders.

On March 7, 1918, the payroll of the Napoleon Motors Company was $300 a week. There were seven new automobiles on the sales floor and the plant could turn out two cars, or trucks, a day.

Through the next couple of years the company tottered like an anemic goat. Now it could pay its bills and now it couldn't. More often than not, it couldn't, and at times it was difficult to get parts with which to assemble the vehicles.

Charles Augustine making a final inspection of his bamboo aircraft in 1910. He and William Campbell, both of Traverse City, began work on the structure in 1909.

It is reasonably certain that the Napoleon automobile and truck held its own with any on the road at that time. Experts said it was well built and reasonably dependable. More could not be said of any car of that day.

In the pleasure car class they built the Chummy Four and the Big Six. In addition, there was another four-cylinder car that was designated only by a

21

number. The Chummy Four came equipped with a motometer—remember them?—and tires, geared to the road, which were guaranteed for six thousand miles. It sold for $1,085 and the Big Six sold for $1,285. Rennie Auto Sales in Traverse City was the district distributor.

In one of the final bursts of enthusiasm to save the company, four experts from the Republic plant at Alma were called in. It was after the arrival of these four men that the big blow fell.

The Napoleon plant was making a truck, the Glidden, for export to Scotland. Crated and on the dock in New York City, sixty-four of these vehicles were awaiting customs clearance. Then an argument about the rate of money exchange arose and local officials fiddled while storage and dockage fees burned the Napoleon financial reserve.

It was after this argument that the final chapter of the plant was written. There were feeble attempts to keep the assembly line going, but it had lost too much financial blood.

Local stockholders awoke one day to find that the pretty certificates they had purchased were worthless. They didn't even have a bankruptcy dividend to show for their investment.

No one was a terrific loser, thanks to the small sales. It wasn't a matter of wiping out a fortune for any one person. However, everyone who did have a spare $10.00 bill in 1918, and invested it in Napoleon stock, did lose it.

Today there is little to prove that there ever was an automobile manufacturing plant in the city. From the files of the *Record-Eagle* copies of order blanks and stock certificates have been uncovered. Here and there, musty in attics, can probably be found other mementos, useless but interesting.

The old factory building has been revamped and is now being used as a city garage. The office building on East Eighth Street was leased to the Zapf Fruit Package Company and later to a trucking concern for offices and dockage. In 1956, it was torn down.

Traverse City missed out as an automobile manufacturing center. But for the failure of the Napoleon Motor Company, Detroit might well be taking a back seat today.

Hannah, Lay and Company

THE ROMANCE of the pine trails and the paths of the "whitewater millionaires" of the lumbering days came to an end in Traverse City history in 1928 when one of its saddest chapters was written.

In that year the Hannah, Lay and Company leased the Hannah, Lay Building to Montgomery Ward and Co. and ended seventy-five years of spectacular service to the community.

When the company ceased operations, there was an undercurrent of deep sentiment manifested by employees who grew old in the service of the company store, a devotion to the organization that was little short of an obsession. Most of them had been with the "Big Store" practically all their working lives, and they wondered how they were going to meet a world in which their old friend would have no part.

"Why, I've worked for the company's store for more than forty years," said George W. Blue, superintendent for nineteen years, when the announcement of the closing was made. "I drove team first, down in the lumber yard. I helped lay brick on this building, back in 1883. When I came into the store, under Smith Barnes, of Port Huron, who was then in the firm, I was required to take up night school work, and given experience in every department. I worked in each one for a year, then repeated the rounds. I have given my life to the company store. And, in all the more than forty years I have worked here, I never took a vacation."

There were one hundred and seven employees in the store when it closed.

"No company in Michigan had a unit that touched the home life of its territory as did the Hannah, Lay and Company store," said Harvey Morrison, credit man for the concern. "With the company it never was a question of profit, but always, 'How much good can we do the community?'" If a man asked for $500 worth of credit, the credit man did not figure how much they were going to make on the deal, but how much good would be done by letting the man have the credit.

The store's history was thrilling and colorful. It probably was the most picturesque and romantic enterprise that ever did business in Michigan.

William W. Smith, for many years an employee of the company, starting as a cabin boy on the company's steamship *Allegheny* in 1865, declared that during the years when the policy of the company was to sell only for cash Perry Hannah personally gave credit to his customers. He dipped into his pocket to pay for what they wanted, letting them repay him instead of charging it on the books to the company.

"I remember back in 1881," Smith said, "when there was a big potato crop, Hannah let the farmers make the profit on what we bought. I was paying 75

The Big Mill, the center of the Hannah, Lay and Company lumbering empire in the Grand Traverse region. It was located where Clinch Park, Traverse City, now stands. In the foreground is the Boardman River.

cents a bushel, and selling them for 85 cents when he told me to give the growers 85 cents and sell for 85.

"'Remember,' Hannah said, 'every cent the farmers make on their farms comes back to us in trade. Give them the profit on the potatoes!'"

Emanuel Wilhelm was in charge of the clothing and dry goods departments, and William Holdsworth was head of the furniture and wallpaper departments when the store closed. Wilhelm had been trained in the business by his father, E. P. Wilhelm, who himself began in the company store on Bay Street and continued in charge of dry goods after the new store was built. Upon his death in 1908, he was succeeded by his son, Emanuel, who completed more than forty years of service in the store. Holdsworth was with the firm more than thirty years. Both were stockholders.

The store had been originally built under Smith Barnes, whose intention was to train the heads of the departments and then sell them the stores, individually. But Barnes died shortly after joining the firm.

At the beginning, Herbert Montague, for many years superintendent of the Masonic Home at Alma, had charge of the grocery department. The hardware was under the direction of John Fowle; the shoes, C. B. Atwood; and dry goods, George Blue.

The Hannah, Lay dock, built for the steamship line in the early seventies, operated as a passenger dock for Traverse City for a number of years after the company closed up. Eli W. Weston was passenger agent. In the days when it and other docks were new, the bayshore was lined with hundreds of cords of wood, brought in by the farmers for the boilers of the steamers. For many years the price was 50 cents a cord. The wood itself was a liability on the farm sites, which were being cleared for homes, and the 50 cents a cord paid for the labor of cutting.

In its infancy, the store was a little log structure on Bay Street, north of the Boardman River. On the shelves were a few bolts of bright colored calico and gingham, red flannel, mackinaw coats for the lumbermen, work clothes, provisions and a small stock of hardware. The provisions were mainly salt pork, molasses, beans, flour, corn meal and sugar. In the original building there was also a real estate office where new residents were sold land on which to build their homes.

The company soon outgrew its log store and the stock was moved across Union Street to a frame building which stood where the old Manistee and Northeastern Railway Depot was later located. This location, too, soon became too small and the first department store in northern Michigan was opened in a new building on the east side of North Union Street and north of the Boardman River, facing what is now Grandview Parkway.

The "departments" in the new location each occupied a separate building with identification across the front of each. On the Union Street side of the Bay Street building the street was "paved" with sawdust which was as smooth as macadam. In 1880, a three-story brick block replaced the last frame structures of the Company. When it was built, it was the last word in retail store architecture. It carried the same line of diversified stock that the old frame store had carried, but all under one roof.

At the west end of the block, banking was done through the Safety Vault Company of Chicago. This bank, begun in the old store in 1856, grew into a great financial institution, the Traverse City State Bank, incorporated in 1892. At that time Perry Hannah was president; his only son, Julius T. Hannah, was vice-president; Samuel Garland was cashier; Howard Irish, paying teller; Leon Titus, receiving teller; George W. Hall, cashier for Hannah, Lay and Company; Charles S. Vader, Jr. and J. C. Sherwood, bookkeepers; and Charles E. Hale, stenographer.

Farmers jockeyed for places along the "big store" front before the advent of the automobile. Oftentimes they bought crackers and cheese from the store and made their lunch hour a social time, discussing current events and the crop outlook.

The new location was the social center of the fast-growing village. Moreover, in time, the farmers who came to settle on the cut-over lands also made it their town "home" as they drove into the settlement with their produce to exchange for wares. As time went on, the company's influence was felt throughout northern Michigan, for it became both the business and social center for the state north of Grand Rapids. Out of this center came great units: the Traverse City State Bank, the old grist mill that burned in 1926, the Park Place Hotel, and a vast real estate business.

From this center, also, was launched a great fleet of ships. First came the sailing vessels which carried lumber to Chicago and brought back provisions and other supplies into the wilderness, then the steamships that built up a gigantic passenger trade.

The first Hannah, Lay sailing ship was the brig *J. Y. Scammon*. She was wrecked on the Manitou Islands. Others were the *Telegraph*, the *Richmond*, the *Sunnyside* and the *Maria Hill*.

Since the waters of Grand Traverse Bay were not charted, the ship masters had to guess their way down the thirty-mile stretch from the mouth of the bay to Traverse City. Old timers tell a story of how the *Richmond* once refused to obey the helm one dark night as she tacked up the bay. Time and again the helm was thrown over, but the boat seemed to be fast. The crew, finally worn down, dropped anchor and went to bed. In the morning they found the schooner's rigging held fast in the branches of a tree.

Then came the palatial steamer *Alleghany*, built in 1865 in Cleveland for the company's lumber trade, but fitted, also, for passengers. The *City of Traverse*, which followed, fell into disrepute after it was sold by the company. It was operated as a gambling boat off Chicago.

Next in turn came the *City of Grand Rapids*, wrecked at the mouth of the Muskegon Channel off the city of Muskegon; then the *Clara Belle*, named after Clarabelle Hannah, the millionaire's daughter; then the *Faxton*, which continued to run as a bay boat long after the peak of the lumber trade had passed. A passenger business grew up and flourished and died.

The sailing ships finally passed from the lakes, and the steamer trade dwindled on the bay. But the two docks built in Traverse City by the Hannah interests remained in use for many years. One handled the coal and lumber business for the firm, the other was later owned by R. Floyd Clinch, of Chicago, son-in-law and last president of the organization over which Perry Hannah once ruled.

From the very beginning, a boarding house was provided for the men employed by the Hannah, Lay and Company, particularly for the unmarried mill hands. As the town grew, the demand for an up-to-date hotel became a necessity. Henry D. Campbell, who later built the first waterworks in Traverse City and, incidentally, in northern Michigan, erected, in 1873, the fifty-room Park Place Hotel, the finest north of Grand Rapids. It was operated by Campbell until 1879, when it was taken over by the Hannah, Lay and Company interests.

In 1881 William O. Holden took charge as manager. A large annex, which increased the rooms to 125, was built in 1880.

The Park Place, a popular summer resort hotel, depended for its year-around trade upon salesmen who pushed on up into the Grand Rapids and Indiana Railway area as far north as Traverse City to make their rounds through Leelanau County by livery team. Across the street from the hotel was a livery barn. The building burned not long after the automobile came into popular use, and on the site there now stands a modern building used as an automobile sales-room and garage. In the days of the horse, the Park Place Hotel owned carriages which met every train.

In 1857, the company built the first grist mill in northern Michigan on the site of the first sawmill. The sawmill had been erected by Horace Boardman on Mill Creek (now Kid's Creek), but Perry Hannah, soon after purchasing the town site, built a new mill on Bay Street, which was remodeled in 1879 and modern machinery was installed. At its peak, it turned out twenty million feet of lumber annually.

Perry Hannah was a red-blooded man with an iron will and a determination to do something worthwhile. He was born on a farm near Erie, Pa., September 22, 1824.

When he was a boy, his father came to Michigan, locating in St. Clair County. Perry joined him at the age of thirteen, leaving school to take up work in the lumber woods with his father. At twenty-one he became a clerk in the dry goods store of John Wells in Port Huron, but before he was twenty-two, he went to Chicago, ripe for adventure. His experience in the woods, especially in rafting logs on tumbling white waters, had put him in fine physical condition. He began work as an office boy for A. Tracy Lay, who, with James Morgan, had a business at Jackson and Canal Streets buying lumber in the harbor by cargo.

In the spring of 1851, Perry Hannah wanted a sawmill of his own. He stood well with Tracy Lay, who encouraged his ambition. Hannah had talked with D. C. Curtis, the engineer who had built the Boardman Mill, and the glowing stories Curtis told of the Grand Traverse region made him decide to head north.

Perry Hannah and William Morgan, accompanied by Captain Harry Board-man, started for the settlement in May of that year aboard the little schooner

28

Venus and, after several days, pulled up at Old Mission. The next day they came to what is now Traverse City. There were a slab dock, a small mill, and a few cheap buildings; Boardman owned two hundred acres of land which he had obtained from the government.

Perry Hannah saw a fortune in the thousands of acres of timber in the region. He traveled ten miles up the river, and, upon returning, told Lay that he had seen around two hundred million feet of marketable lumber. For $4,500 they bought the mill, the few buildings and the two hundred acres which had been platted for a village. That was the real beginning of Traverse City.

They organized the firm of Hannah, Lay and Company, with Perry Hannah as the guiding hand. Lay looked after the Chicago interests, which were then considerable, but which were later greatly increased to include the Chicago Board of Trade Building. For a few years the two men changed places summers, Lay spending six months of the warm season in Traverse City and Hannah staying in Chicago during the same period.

From the first the firm was successful. Everything Hannah touched turned to money. Thrifty by nature in his habits, he set out to wrest a fortune from the wilderness—and won. Adventure colored his every move. As a youth he rafted logs through tumbling white waters. When he had become a millionaire, he rode logs down the Boardman River, and over the dam just to show the "boys" how it was done in the "good old days" or just to entertain the Fourth of July crowds that stood on the banks cheering. For several years he was known as the "white-water millionaire riverman," competing with Jack Rennie, Sr., and other younger daredevils.

Hannah had a dignity of bearing that made him a distinguished figure wherever he went. Invariably he wore a Prince Albert coat and a plug hat. He taught his children to revere the simple things of life, training them in the discipline of self denial.

Perry Hannah built his first home on a site where he could watch his ships, laden with supplies, come sailing down the bay. Today, a wholesale grocery house obstructs the view, and the house itself was wrecked nearly thirty years ago. It was not until his family was grown and one of them married that he built his palatial home on Sixth Street, which still stands. He also built a cottage for himself at what is now 233 Bay Street. In this little cottage by the shore,

Hannah raised his two children and entertained his wealthy partners on their visits to Traverse City.

To Perry Hannah, more than to any other man, Traverse City owes its early prosperity. Yet he was modest; not much that went into the making of the city bears his name. Its beautiful lake bears the name of Boardman, for it was Henry Boardman who started the lumbering. The river which empties into Grand Traverse Bay, the "white water" of the old days, was also named for the Boardmans. Today it is a sedate stream through the city. But there are Hannah Park, donated to the city by its builder, and an avenue named for the Hannah family, and there were the Hannah Rifles of Spanish American War days.

Hannah named the village Grand Traverse City, but the "grand" was dropped at the suggestion of a clerk in Washington, D.C., in 1853, when Albert Tracy Lay, junior partner in the firm, tried to obtain a postoffice for the town.

Perry Hannah and his wife, Anna Flint, of Chicago, are buried in Oakwood Cemetery, the forty-acre plot he gave to the city many years ago.

A Century of Learning

IT WAS a chilly day in November 1851, when the schooner *Madeline* rounded Old Mission Point, Peninsula Township, and headed past the bight which juts out to form Bowers Harbor. Aboard were five young men who intended to winter in the region aboard ship, but rather than while away their time in idleness, they decided to improve their education.

Getting to work immediately, they partitioned off a section of the hold of the *Madeline* for a galley, a sash was set at a forty-five degree angle over the after hatch for light, and a door was cut through the cabin so it could be used as a school room. S. E. Wait was engaged as teacher at a salary of $20.00 a month and classes began in the first school in the Grand Traverse region except for the strictly missionary instruction among the Indians at Old Mission.

That first school enrolled the three Fitzgerald brothers, William, Michael, and John; William Bryce; and a man named Edward Chambers, who gave his services as a cook for his tuition.

The next step toward the establishment of an institution of formal education was in the winter of 1853 at Wequetong (Head-of-the-Bay) which is now Traverse City. With the big Hannah, Lay and Company mill running full blast there was a gradual influx of families with youngsters who needed reading, writing and arithmetic. Dr. D. C. Goodale, who came to Traverse City to manage the company boarding house, arranged to have his daughter, Helen, then fifteen years old, employed as the first teacher. Perry Hannah, then a leading member of the community, agreed that if the parents failed to meet the obligation of salary, he would make up the deficit.

Probably no more accurate description of this first school building will ever be given than the one written by Mrs. Thomas Hitchcock in 1899. Mrs. Hitch-

31

cock was formerly Helen Goodale, the pioneer teacher. Here is her description:

"The path along the river wandered away from every sound, the hush of the forest ending only on the shore of the bay, out and in and around the wide oaks, which, grouping like hedgeways, rose to the branches of the tall Norways. Long aisles, plain pillared aisles, decorated here and there with oak screen . . . under which the river ran so swiftly. Beyond and between the pines on Squaw Peninsula glistened the bay.

"I suddenly came to a little space, green with its wild grass, enclosed with the oaken hedge, save on the north its open front revealed the river.

"In the space stood a little cabin, its closed door giving it a silent, deserted appearance, harmonizing so well with the unbroken silence . . . ."

The story so often repeated is that the cabin was formerly a stable. Even the name of the teamster who kept his horses housed in it appears to be known. However, about that, here is what Mrs. Hitchcock has to say: "An old settler informed me that the old cabin was built for a family to live in and was not used as a stable. It was there when I came here and that is all I know of it previous to 1853."

It was a dilapidated old building and the floor was loose and open. On one occasion the teacher and her little class were terrified when a snake appeared through one of the large cracks in the floor.

Following her first years as a school teacher, Miss Goodale went to Chicago to study. In her absence, the school was taught by Helen Gamon, a sister of a Mrs. Holton. The second winter, classes were held in the Boardman Boarding House. The old boarding house was located close to the first sawmill on what is now Kid's Creek, near the present residence of Gene Stark in the 100 block, North Division Street.

On May 11, 1854, the first school district was formed, and the first meeting of the school board was held in the Hannah, Lay and Company store on May 17, 1854. Alvin Smith was named moderator. David Goodale was elected director, and Thomas Cutler became the assessor.

The school terms of 1854-55 were again conducted in the old boarding house and in September 1855, the board voted $200 for the purpose of building a school house. The winter of 1855 saw classes held in an old Front Street house, in the 200 block, East Front Street.

During the following summer, a new school was erected on property later occupied by the Park Place Hotel Annex which was razed in the fall of 1956. A second building was erected in 1869, the first building having been moved to a new and undisclosed site for use as a primary classroom.

In 1861, there were 122 children in growing Traverse City, forty-eight of whom were enrolled in classes. That summer, school was taught by Belle Hannah, sister of the prominent lumberman and business leader, Perry Hannah.

In 1867, three teachers were employed. Enrollment was 130 students.

In 1894, the city boasted seven public schools and twelve teachers. The census of 1893 listed 868 school-age children in the district.

The growth of the schools in the city was a sign of the healthy growth of the community. Such names as Saylor, Anderson, Roberts, Saxton and Nixon have come down through the years as pioneers in the educational advances of the city. Today, there are six modern public grade schools, three denominational grade schools and one public high school. A total of 153 teachers are employed in the public schools, educating 3,748 students.

Using the present basic salary of $4,800 a year for a teacher holding an M.A. degree as a standard, Helen Goodale would have to teach 415 years to earn one modern year's teaching income. Of course, Miss Goodale didn't have to have an automobile and she got her room and board as part of her contract; moreover, in her own words, "The summer I spent teaching at Traverse City was the happiest one in my life."

33

Northwestern Michigan College

TO MEET the complete education needs
of the descendants of the pioneers of the Grand Traverse region has always been
a long-standing dream among the area's leading citizens and educators.

Prior to 1951 it had only been the most wishful thinking but in that year,
through the providence of generous residents, Northwestern Michigan College
was founded, thus providing a facility where youth could receive university
preparation, terminal education and semi-professional training at moderate cost
and in familiar surroundings. Classes were held in vacant, city-owned buildings at
the Traverse City Airport, giving the new institution a grip on reality. Beginning
with only sixty-five students and a skeleton staff, the school immediately began to
expand. Not satisfied with the cramped quarters, the residents of the community,
sparked by a few leaders, made ambitious plans to build a modern school.

Gifts from the public, fund raising programs by students and organizations,
state-matching monies, and many other minor dollar-raising activities contributed to the modern college in the center of the Grand Traverse region.

In all activities, there was a dominant figure. Les Beiderman, owner of a radio
and television station, himself deprived of higher education in his youth, led the
drive. His dreams, often considered impractical or impossible, became reality.

Today, in 1958, Northwestern Michigan College is accredited by the
Michigan Commission on College Accreditation. It has turned out many successful students and its facilities are still growing rapidly. From the original student
body of 65, it arrived at an enrollment of 457 in 1957. Its laboratory equipment,
its staff, its counseling service—and its future—are excellent.

The new college buildings are located in a section of virgin white pine on the
east side of Traverse City, a fitting site for an institution which is truly pioneer.

FEW
REMAIN

The village, located in the southern part of Grand Traverse County, started with the arrival of the Grand Rapids and Indiana Railway early in 1873. Within a few years the village was known from one end of the railway district to the other as Hell. A lumber-jack could go into a ticket office in South Bend and ask for a ticket to Hell and the agent would turn around to the slotted rack, take out a Walton one-way and hand it through the wicket.

No Longer an Outpost

THE GRAND Traverse region, once an isolated outpost, is today only hours from great metropolitan centers. Chicago, New York, Detroit, are almost suburban. Letters mailed today are in Los Angeles tomorrow, in Europe the day after.

It was not always thus. H. D. Campbell, first assistant postmaster in the Grand Traverse region, also the man who distributed the first official mail in the region, wrote down some of his memories before the turn of the century. Here is his report of the early activities and the establishment of the first postoffice in this region.

"This part of Michigan, north of the Muskegon River, was, prior to 1850, an unbroken wilderness, with but one postoffice, then known as the Grand Traverse postoffice, located at what is now Old Mission, without any post route to connect with any mail service; the nearest office on the south was Croton, on the Muskegon River, directly south one hundred and twenty miles, and

Twelve Grand Traverse area pioneers, 1897. Pictured left to right, with their respective ages at the time of the photograph, are: Joseph Knizek, 78; Reuben Goodrich, 78; J. W. Robertson, 73; E. P. Ladd, 78; H. E. Steward, 71; Samuel Anderson, 78; Perry Hannah, 73; John A. Cook, 75; William Holdsworth, 81; Dominie Dunn, 77; Philip Secor, 72; and Thomas Brockway, 74. Their names appear again and again in the early records of the Grand Traverse region.

Mackinaw on the north, about one hundred miles distance. An old and well defined Indian trail between these points over which the Indians were sent from the Upper Peninsula once during the close of navigation for all mail matter that might accumulate at Croton for this north county, and all mail for this neighborhood [Traverse City] was carried past us to Grand Traverse postoffice, twenty miles away.

"To illustrate the convenience of mail facilities here in the early days a little experience of the writer will explain.

"I came here in the fall of 1852, about the time of the presidential election that fall, and about the first of March the following spring a squad of twenty Indians and as many dogs came from the Upper Peninsula on their way to Croton for the United States mail and in due time returned, the Indians upon snow shoes, with packs of mail and camping outfit, in Indian file, thus packing the snow into a well beaten path for the dog trains to follow. Usually three to six dogs are harnessed in tandem to a sledge similar in form to our toboggan sledges, with mail bags, supplies, etc., bound to them. One Indian follows in the rear to see that all is well as the train a mile or more in extent moves along forward.

"On this occasion the mail for Traverse City was carried also and distributed at the Grand Traverse postoffice, and it happened that Ann Dakin, a domestic at the Boarding House (now Pangborn Hotel), was visiting at the Old Mission. So she received the mail for this place, (over a hundred pounds), strapped it on her back and brought it to the head of the bay. In this mail we received the news that Gen. Franklin Pierce had been elected President of the United States, and was on the fourth of March duly inaugurated into the high office in Washington.

"While we received mail but once during the close of navigation, we frequently had opportunities of sending letters out to kindred and kind friends by some person from the north on his way over the trail to the outside world, who would take our letters for fifty cents apiece and mail them. These chances were gratifying, though at times expensive. Upon one occasion I gave a man a ten dollar gold piece to take a box containing a present to my mother and express it to Muskegon. You may query now how I could trust a stranger with so valuable a package. My answer is, we did not have dishonest neighbors in those days. All believed in honesty as the best policy.

"Traverse City postoffice was established in 1853 with post route from Muskegon up the lake shore via Whitehall, Ludington, Manistee to Sleeping Bear, thence through the woods to Traverse City and over the trail to Grand Traverse [now Old Mission] with semi-monthly mail service.

"The late Dr. D. C. Goodale was appointed postmaster with the writer assistant. The doctor in order to qualify, in company with his bondsmen, W. M. McKillip, now of Muskegon, and the late Thomas Cutler, went to Old Mission, a two days journey over the trail. During their absence the first mail arrived, being packed through from Manistee by one Peter Greenksey, a faithful Indian mail carrier, and the writer had the honor of distributing the first United States mail in the Traverse City postoffice. The mailbag contained seven letters and several newspapers for this office. The cost of transportation over this route was $400 a year. The revenue of the office the first year was $3.00, all of which was expended for an office stamp.

" 'To the victor belong the spoils' so in President Lincoln's administration Yours Truly was appointed successor to succeed Dr. D. C. Goodale in the post-office. At this time the revenue of the office had increased to about $150.00 a year. A year later, in 1862, having become interested in the establishment of post routes, postoffices and mail service in the northern counties, I resigned my commission and gave special attention to the increased demand for more and better mail facilities.

"During these early years our mails were carried by trusty Indians. The only precaution taken was a charge not to get drunk while in the mail service. We used to subject them to swear to kiss the bible, (as often as otherwise would be a pocket diary) that he would keep sober while making a trip. I have yet to learn of the first violation of this solemn obligation.

"For many years from 1851 some of our letters were brought to us during the season of navigation from Chicago by lumber vessels or steam craft making regular trips between Chicago and Traverse City, a source of convenience to many living in this vicinity.

"An incident in this connection in 1862, while I was yet postmaster, that has never been made a public matter, may not be out of place to mention now, shows how contemptible an evil-disposed person can be under certain circumstances.

38

"This person had reported to the postoffice department that boats making regular trips between Chicago and Traverse City were then, and had been, carrying United States mail unauthorized between these points, and papers and instructions were sent to me as postmaster to investigate and arrest the officers and owners of the boats handling mail without authority.

"As a matter of fact everybody living here was more or less accommodated by this gratuitous act on the part of the boats' officers and owners in question.

"No person except it might have been myself could have any well founded grievance from this cause and that only in so far as it might affect my commission in the postoffice business. So I concluded to assume the role of judge and jury and pocket the papers and keep mum unless forced to take action at some future time, and the papers have never been served to this day.

"The first daily mail service was put in operation by the writer between Big Rapids and Traverse City, via Sherman in 1870, requiring four days time for a round trip. In 1873 mails were brought by rail from Clam Lake (Cadillac) by my agents, thus giving us daily mails from Detroit and Chicago in twenty to twenty-four hours in place of three days per contract schedule time.

"Since 1874 much of our mail service has been performed by railroad service bringing our mails several times daily. All of this has helped to increase the business of the Traverse City postoffice, which is second to none of the many offices located north of the Muskegon River today."

Vinegar Pie

SO YOU, Mrs. Modern Housewife, think you had a rough day? You struggled out of bed at the obnoxious hour of 8:30 a.m. and plugged in the electric percolator and the electric toaster. You opened the front door a wee bit and snatched up the quart of milk and the morning paper.

At 9:30 you turned off the electric dishwasher, ran the last of the kitchen refuse through the garbage grinder, turned on the radio or television and took five to recoup your shattered nerves.

After a day like that, who wouldn't be worn in body, be crabbed and snarling at hubby, and bark at the youngsters.

But things were different back in the nineteenth century when Mrs. Frank Flarity, Manistee, cooked in the lumber camps of the Grand Traverse region. In those roaring days a lumberjack worked from sunup to sundown and was always ready for supper call.

Mrs. Flarity began her day at 5:30, when she cooked for the Buckley and Douglas Lumbering Company at Twin Mountain camp, Nessen City. Three times a day she prepared a meal for sixty-five healthy appetites. Of course she had a couple of flunkies, sometimes called "cookees" by the fellows who write romantic pieces about the camps.

Twice each week she baked thirty-five loaves of bread and three hundred and fifty buns. Every forenoon she baked a fifty-pound keg of molasses cookies and a fifty-pound keg of white cookies. (The kegs were probably former nail containers.) Every other day of the week she turned out a keg of fried cakes and every morning before daylight she had eighteen pies out of the oven.

For twenty years, she followed the camps. She boiled and baked enough

40

beans to feed a small navy. Side pork and beef steak were common bill-of-fare and now and then a little venison—there was always lots of meat in the camps where she worked.

Breakfast in a lumber camp was one to bolster a weakened constitution. "Most generally," Mrs. Flarity has said, "we had warmed up 'taters and salt pork for breakfast, along with all the pancakes the men could eat. And coffee for breakfast, lots of it, boiled in a big pot and poured black and scalding hot."

"You know," she remarks, "there's more to warming up 'taters than most women know. You have to get the meat fryings just so hot—almost smoking— before the 'taters are put in the iron skillet. Then you chop them with a tin can until they are pretty fine. Brown them and turn them two or three times and they are fine, not at all like the soggy ones you get in a restaurant."

Mrs. Christine Nelson, another lumber camp cook, was a sprite of a lady. She saw the pine retreat before the sawyers and axmen and cooked to match their great appetites. She is a past master at preparing pig hocks and beans, also rutabagas, fried or boiled.

Making maple sugar in the Grand Traverse region in the spring of 1885. The maple sap, as is shown here, had to be boiled, and evaporated, for hours. One barrel of sap produced only a single gallon of syrup, which was often the only sweet available to the pioneers.

Dessert? Of course! There was always an ample supply of prune pie, raisin pie, dried apple pie and, once in a while, a little lemon pie if the cook could get some lemon extract.

There were no recipes to go by when one cooked for a lumber camp. One just took a pinch of this and a scoop of that, a little fat for shortening, and a dab of something else and—presto!—good, wholesome food.

One of the most colorful cooks of the region was Mrs. Mary Conklin, Traverse City. She went to work as a flunky on a wannigan at the age of twelve. To the boys of the pine, a wannigan was a woods scow—a floating eating house. The first wannigan on which Mrs. Conklin worked ferried between Elk Rapids and Eastport, tending the appetites of the crews cutting for the famous Dexter and Noble firm.

The appetites of the seagoing lumberjacks were no different. It was the same story. A bushel of cookies baked before daylight; thousands of fried cakes; beans, bacon, fat salt pork from a barrel—all staples of the lumber era.

Another item of which the men were fond was cornmeal mush. For breakfast, it served as a cereal. One cooks it slow and thin and serves it with milk and brown sugar. One can also cook it a little longer, pour it in a bread pan and let it cool, then slice and fry it crispy brown. With a dab of butter and a bit of maple syrup, it is a dish for a king.

"Oh, yes," Mrs. Conklin recalls, "just mix in a few handfuls of meat cracklin's with the mush when you are cooking it and it makes it a lot more tasty."

From yeast to oven, Mrs. Conklin, like scores of other cooks through the northland, provided her own ingredients for baking. Wheat was milled in local establishments, and she raised her own hops. In recalling the use of yeast in those early days, she said it was "kept alive," as long as two years. "You just take some boiled 'taters," she explained, "jam them good. You steep the hops just right and mix them, and there you have it."

The Swedish and Norwegian lumberjacks liked their thin, odorous sourdough pancakes. The worse they smelled, the better they liked them. Others liked "raised cakes"; some wanted cornmeal in the batter; and others liked buck-wheat, especially in the winter because, they explained, buck-wheat was "heatin'."

No story of food and appetites would be complete without mention of an old favorite! Vinegar Pie, a lumber camp standby. Is there a housewife today who could make one? Mrs. Russell Wood, Kalkaska, cooked them for a number of camps over the northern part of the state. The last camp was the Tindle and Jackson camp at Pellston.

Just in case you want to whip up a little Vinegar Pie, here is her method:

1¼ cups granulated sugar

1¼ cups boiling water

¼ cup vinegar

¼ cup cornstarch

Dash of nutmeg (if you have it).

Stir the ingredients together and cook until clear and thick. Stir half the mixture into three beaten egg yolks; combine mixture again; place entire filling back on wood range for one minute, add a tablespoon of butter and pour into a baked shell. If you wish to be fancy, just in case the girls are going to drop in, make the usual meringue. (But lumberjacks were happy to have the pie without the fringe on top.)

The call to meals varied according to the location of the camps, the whims of the cook, or the will of the workmen. Sometimes a great iron triangle struck by a heavy iron was the signal. Or, it was a long dinner horn with a call like that of a mating bull moose. It could have been a trumpet call through the barrel of a twelve gauge shotgun. It could have been the simple expedient of the lumberjacks looking at a dollar pocket watch. One thing was certain, no one was ever late for a meal.

Meal time was for eating. The men had their own places at the long plank tables and they kept them. Heaven help the new man who got in the wrong place. There was no idle chatter at the tables. "Pass the 'taters." "Some bread." "Hand me the butter." That was the extent of the conversation.

Louis Nelson, Keystone (Grand Traverse County), was one of the lads who wielded the pancake turner and fired a green wood stove. He, like scores of others, was one of the "long hour" boys of the woods camps.

But the ladies, bless 'em, were in there in major numbers. They didn't have any electric toasters or dishwashers; they had no vacuum coffee makers or electric mixers. They had ambition, endurance and skill. On top of all that, they had long hours. A fifteen-hour day was not unusual, but an eight-hour day was rare indeed.

A Forgotten Industry

THOUGH in the past century the manufacture of high-quality bricks in the Grand Traverse region bid fair to become an industry of large proportions, it has become a nearly forgotten trade. There are not too many folks remaining who worked in the old Markham yard or kiln, to mention one of the largest and most properous.

This particular yard made countless thousands of high-grade bricks at its kilns near Greilickville. In fact, the Traverse City State Bank, the Masonic Building, the Hannah and Lay Building (Montgomery Ward) and a majority of the state hospital buildings were built with Markham bricks. Originally, during the hospital construction, the bricks were hauled from the Greilickville plant to the hospital by teams. Six teams were used to keep the masons busy. Later a special train was used to haul the bricks.

This story has little to do with the Markham kilns but with the pioneer pits which proved that local clay and sand could be used in the manufacture of building material.

The first pit was opened near Keystone, seven miles south of Traverse City, about the year 1882. Charles Hunter and Jack Baumbaugh, enterprising adventurers, examining the clay in the Keystone area, decided it was perfect. They began construction of a building and the installation of a kiln.

In a short time their factory was producing solid bricks in both white and red. The bricks were known to the trade as "slush brick," sometimes as "slop brick." The method of manufacture consisted of mixing a small amount of sand with the clay, forming the bricks into molds, steam drying them, and then baking them in a kiln.

There is no record of how many bricks were produced in their plant. It is pretty definite, however, that a majority of the output was loaded on cars and shipped by rail to southern Michigan markets.

Hunter and Baumbaugh erected a boarding house across the old sand trail, east of the Boardman River. The employees took their meals there, as did some of the lumbermen in the region and crewmen from the Beitner mill.

The Hunter and Baumbaugh pit operated for about three years, as near as records can establish. Louis Nelson, now nearing his eighty-eighth birthday (1956), worked in the plant when he was fourteen years of age. He recalls most of the activities.

The H & B brick kiln was the first in northern Michigan, but not the last. Major Newcomb, no one seems to know his first name, bought the holdings and it closed shortly thereafter.

The next brick manufacturing enterprise at the Keystone location was the Traverse City Brick Company which began operations in the "year of the big snow." This was a stock company and many local pioneer names were associated with it. Such names as Bartak, Thirlby and Wilhelm were listed as stockowners. The enterprise was engineered by Charles Emmerson and Cal Smith.

More pretentious and larger than the H & B kiln, the Traverse City Brick Company was located just north of the pioneer pits. A rail siding was laid, drying sheds erected and a large steam boiler mounted on cement foundations.

There is no record of the number of bricks manufactured at this plant other than that the output was "terrific." Both red and white, solid surface bricks were turned out.

The steel rails of the old siding were removed many years ago, but the ties, rotting and nearly overgrown, are still evident about a quarter of a mile away from the Traverse City side of Keystone Corners. The cement foundations on which the giant boiler rested are still in evidence, and a great pile of shale and broken brick can still be seen from the paved highway.

The road to the clay pit is not yet completely overgrown and, with minimum effort one can imagine carts hauling clay and sand to the mixing bins and steam pouring out of the drying sheds.

After manufacture ceased, the Traverse City Brick Company holdings were eventually sold. Several reasons for the liquidation of this company have been advanced, ranging from competitive operations farther south to poor quality

46

bricks. The latter excuse certainly doesn't stand up for many homes built of Keystone brick are still in excellent condition.

The bricks on hand when the factory was wrecked were sold to Hannah, Lay and Company and were used in the construction of one of the buildings at the Armour Estate, Long Lake. William Dill, who bought the holdings for salvage, sold the lumber from the old plant for boxcar lining; the boiler was loaded on a flat car at Slights Siding and shipped south.

But the closing of the Hunter and Baumbaugh and the Traverse City Brick Company enterprises was not the end of brick production in this area. The Markham plant continued to operate; moreover, in 1937, the Holmes brick plant opened on the river road about two miles beyond Slights Siding. A. L. Robbins, who had worked earlier in the Traverse City Brick Company kilns, accepted a position with the Holmes outfit. About 150,000 bricks were turned out before production ceased.

Artesian water for manufacture is still available and, who knows, someday there may be a revival of the old industry.

Pictures of both of the Keystone manufactories have been found in private collections. Photos of the Markham yard have not been preserved as far as is known. The Holmes building, fast rotting away, is still in evidence on the river road.

The Beitner Mill

THERE'S hardly a man now alive who remembers the operation of the William Beitner mill which thrived before the turn of the century. It was called a "chair factory," and specialized in dowels, spindles and chair bottoms. The mill was located on a little creek, known as Beitner Creek, about seven miles south of Traverse City, and was one of the largest of its kind in the state.

The exact date when the mill began operation is not known but Lewis Miller, whose stepfather was one of the first cookees for the crew, believes it was about 1888. The mill turned out countless thousands of board feet of lumber before going into the furniture parts business.

William Beitner was the main figure in the enterprise but his older brother, August, was also involved. Later, August sold his interest to Wash Pound and invested in a saloon which stood in the 400 block of East Front Street, Traverse City.

The factory operated before the present rails were laid for the Chesapeake and Ohio Railway. Dowels and other parts were hauled by team to the siding at Keystone where they were loaded onto Grand Rapids and Indiana Railway cars. The entire output was shipped to a penal institution in the southern part of the state for assembly and finishing.

When the plant was first started, lumber was cut from nearby acreage. As this source became depleted, logs were hauled from as far away as the Silver Lake area.

Most of the chair seats were made from sound beech, and the rest of the products were turned out of maple, oak, cherry, birch and some elm. Bending was done in a steam kiln, and the mill was water powered. The mill pond is somewhat silted now because the mill closed down over a half century ago, in 1904. The Beitner enterprise then moved to Traverse City and a mill was erected on the shores of Boardman Lake at a point just south of the present Chesapeake and Ohio Depot. It was in operation at the same time the Oval Wood Dish factory was hitting its fastest pace.

The chair factory at Beitner cut about ten thousand feet of hardwood a day at peak production. Landowners received $2.50 per thousand feet for the logs, which had to be clean. The woodsmen would fell a tree and cut to the first knots (limbs) and stop. If there was the sign of a shake in the butt or a bit of decayed heartwood, the logs were left in the woods to be burned.

The Beitner School, still standing and until 1957 in use, was built by Tom Whaley. Mary Robinson and Lina Hager were the first teachers. Mary Robinson walked about four miles, night and morning, to bring booklearning to the children of the pioneers in the community. For her work, she received $20.00 a month during the school year.

The old chair factory was dismantled a little at a time, but some of the old buildings fell to ruin and were burned.

There are very few folk now living who can recall accurately the happenings of those days when wood chips dropped from the ancient lathes and the steam bays hissed and leaked, while the spindles and dowels were being prepared for the benders.

Pete Engstrom, who worked two years as setter in the factory, recalled many of the names of that day. His father, Gustav Engstrom, was head sawyer for some time.

Known all over the region were such men as Jack and Frank Yenish, Charlie Weidman, John Kreitz, Barney McGill, Jack Rennie, Aaron and William Dyke, Gotleib Miller, Ira Blood and Jim McGarry, all of whom worked at the William Beitner factory, an indication that the best of the woodsmen were on the payroll.

The Beitners lived in a pleasant home on the edge of the backwater near the mill. The frame of the home was rebuilt into a modern house a few years ago and still stands. Mrs. Beitner, an ardent gardener, had running water for irrigation. A hydraulic ram in the creek forced water into a tank high above the property. The place where the tank stood can still be seen on the south side of the present highway on top of a hill.

The Plains—Rich in History

IN THE plains area southeast of Traverse City, between a point where Hobbs Highway hits the Supply Road and east to Tin Can Corners, there are at least a dozen roads leading off to the left. Today they are mostly sand trails, often grown over by red oak brush or jack pine. There was a day, however, when every one of those trails led to a Hannah, Lay and Company logging camp, and Camp Five was one of the largest. It was located just north of Perch Lake, now Strombolus Lake, and a railroad, built by Cobb and Mitchell of Cadillac cut diagonally from northeast to southwest across the plains.

A visitor to the area would never suspect that in 1875 there was a roaring lumber camp there. Careful search has located the old foundation of the bunkhouse and cook shanty. Great timbers, now rotted to dust, can be traced in the earth. A few rods away the old Swede holes, marking the rail location, can still be found.

Dates of the operation of Camp Five are vague. None of the old lumbermen and woodsmen living know exactly when the "big cut" was made. It is reasonable to believe that the first operation started in 1870 or close thereto.

Frank Samels, who died in 1956, said that in 1871 an early breakup prevented the workmen from getting the logs to the Boardman River and a half million board feet were lost. The gather was later fired to get the logs out of the way. This incident took place before he was old enough to remember, but he heard it from other woodsmen. He recalled, however, such men as John Gillis,. who was a walking boss for the Hannah and Lay interests in the woods. Frank Smith, known in the woods as "One-eyed" Smith and "Cock-eyed" Smith because he lost an eye in his youth, was another of the men who worked in and around

Camp Five as a boss. After Smith came a foreman named Oscar Simpson, later sheriff of Grand Traverse County.

The timber was cut and skidded out to the road and, during the late winter and spring, was hauled by sled to the big rollway on the Boardman River. The rollway was located above what is now Brown Bridge Dam and the evidence of its use can still be seen.

No estimate was ever made of the amount of timber cut and marketed through Camp Five. A large portion of it was shipped to Chicago and some was moved to the east coast.

The oldtimers say that only the choice logs were considered worth floating down the river to the big Hannah and Lay mill on the shore of the west arm of Grand Traverse Bay. If a tree was felled and the butt was hollow or shakey, it was left to rot, or, more likely, to be burned by the many fires which swept over the plains area.

One of the characters who worked at Camp Five was a big bulk of a man who arrived from Cadillac way. The boss called him Eric the Swede and no one made a record of his last name. He had one arm and hired out as a sawyer. Eric the Swede never asked any favors on the job and could out-saw and out-chop almost any other man in the camp. The only money he drew during that winter in the early 1880's was enough to buy tobacco, felt boots and a little whiskey for "medicinal purposes." One exception, however, was the last time any of the lumberjacks ever saw the big, good-natured blond. He borrowed five dollars from one of his co-workers and headed for Traverse City. It was reported he became uproariously drunk in one of the saloons. That was the only report. He never returned to camp, not even to pick up his personal belongings. Somewhere on the old Hannah, Lay and Company books there is a cash balance due Eric the Swede.

Interested parties are planning to erect a marker on the site of old Camp Five. For future generations the site, unmarked, has no meaning; marked, it will live on.

Only a small handful remember old "Dibbie," the donkey narrow gauge, which wheezed through the plains. Even the stumps of the hardwood and pine have returned to dust and the lumbering empire of Hannah and Lay has vanished.

Old timers who worked the camps—Frank Samels, Oliver Pray, Albert

Hammond, Will Johnson—carried the romance of the pine and the hardwood in their minds. Most of the old woodsmen are logging in the spirit world and only a few are alive to record the facts.

Today a maze of unmarked trails presents a challenge to an adventurous spirit. Thousands of acres of rolling land, criss-crossed by little-used roads, makes it possible for the inexperienced woodsman to become lost within a few miles of the city of Traverse City.

For example, if you take the fork to the left at Coffee Pot Swing you will end up at the Kermit French property with its modern home, deep in the jack pine slash. On the other hand, you can take the right fork and arrive at the Gene Knight property at Kingsley. If you wish to be more confused, take the Death Valley path, about a mile and a half long, and you will reach the E. A. Scharman property, one of the oldest farmsteads in the Grand Traverse region.

A person might well wonder where Coffee Pot Swing is located. Anyone who is familiar with the plains country has probably passed it a score of times. On an ancient white pine stump there stands an old coffee pot. Bullet riddled by restless huntsmen, the old pot has been on the stump for more than a quarter of a century. It was placed there by Rudolf Paziener, a resident of the area for the past thirty-five years and known to thousands of people for his Ranch Rudolph. In giving directions to the confusing criss-cross of roads and trails, it was common over the years to say: "Go to the coffee pot and swing left (or right)."

The plains area is not the barren wasteland it was even as recently as a quarter of a century ago. It is rapidly becoming a rolling timberland, studded with markers of historical interest and a veritable warehouse of interesting lore. It would take a guest, accompanied by a guide, of course, at least a week to see all the points of interest the length of the Boardman River, which cuts much of its way through the slash land.

The old Scharman home is an example of the pioneer spirit which fought a losing battle against nature and sandy soil. The old log cabin, located in Section 20, Union Township, is now a shambles. Its logs, once fastened with wooden pegs, are falling apart and the roof has fallen in. But it was here that Fred Scharman dared to rear his family of twelve children. It was once an elaborate farm home and saw a period of prosperity when descendants of the pioneer family operated a turkey and duck farm. A more recent home stands in this isolated section and is kept in reasonable repair by its present owner, E. A. Scharman, Honor, who is reforesting the property.

Scores of regional people have wandered across Section 19 and found the only cemetery in the entire Union Township. A lone grave, deep in the reforested area, marks the last resting place of Emma L. Northrup, who died at the age of six and was buried on the Northrup farm property. The tiny grave, cared for by relatives and strangers alike, bears a quotation on one side and the name and date of death on the other. The verse inscribed on the stone is familiar to those who have read the famous old poet's "There is a reaper whose name is death."

Where the Northrups lived and dreamed of security, there now remains only a dim outline of the old home where rotted timbers are being overgrown with Norway and jack pine. A deep pit marks the site of the small barn with its root cellar. The last of the buildings was moved when Brown Bridge Dam was constructed.

Too, few folks know about Hog Ranch Number Two. And, on the other hand, who would be so bold as to venture into the hog raising business in the plains area? It was George Upthegrove who thought it would work. His elaborate system of hydrants and underground pipes still remains as a monument to his enterprise. Water for the system was secured from a deep well, wind operated, and the water was stored in a large cement tank which still stands. The remains of the project are in Section 18, Union Township.

Old "witness trees" have been dead these many years and a few of the stumps can be found bearing the survey data, which were so all-important in another day.

Logging trails criss-cross through the plains territory and in some places, railroad grades wind like long serpents through the second growth. On the banks of the Boardman River can be seen the worn rollways and the skid roads where log butts ploughed the earth.

To the stranger, the plains are merely extensive acres and long miles of desolation. To the folks who know, there is pioneer hope and an indomitable courage behind every stump and on every hill and knoll which still shows the scars of a crude plowshare. The gnarled apple trees, which remain on many of the pioneer farms, and the rotted fenceposts, which once marked domain, are witness to the courage which has helped make the Grand Traverse region what it is today.

Interlochen

LONG before the white man came with his axe and railroad, a peaceful tribe of Indians inhabited two villages on the shores of two beautiful lakes in Grand Traverse County. Between Lake Wahbekaness (Water Lingers), formerly Duck Lake, and Lake Wahbekanetta (Water Lingers Again), formerly Green Lake, ran a small river and from Lake Wahbekanetta to Lake Michigan ran a larger river, the Betsie River—named after Mrs. Betsie Monro, a pioneer woman of the area. Between these two lakes, on a sandy ridge less than a quarter mile wide in places, grew a most beautiful forest of white and Norway pine.

One Indian village was located on the west shore of Lake Wahbekaness, where the Walter Hastings Nature Museum now stands. The other was located on the south shore of Lake Wahbekanetta, near where the village of Karlin is now located. At times there must have been strife between them because a great many flint war arrows and spear heads have been found at a point midway between them where a deep gulley divides the forest.

During the last half of the nineteenth century the white man came with his railroads, axes and sawmills, to ravish the forests and ship lumber to help rebuild the burned-out city of Chicago. The Pere Marquette ran its railroad past the north end of the two lakes and the Manistee and Northeastern Railroad, primarily a lumber road, ran its line right through the pine forest between the lakes. Where the two railroads crossed, the village of Interlochen (between the lakes) sprang up.

Logs cut from the shores of Green Lake were floated down the Betsie River to the lake port of Frankfort for processing and shipping. Logs cut from the shores of Duck Lake were loaded on lumber trains of the Manistee and Northeastern Railroad. To facilitate getting these logs to the railroad, the lumber company built a dam near the railroad river crossing and dug a ditch from the lake through which a steam tugboat hauled rafts of logs to the point of loading.

Settlers objected to raising the level of the lake, but their objections were ignored. A water wheel was installed at the dam and plans made for generating electric current, but the settlers ended that project by dynamiting the dam. All this happened before 1906.

Were it not for the fact that Edward Buckley, president of the Buckley and Douglas Lumber Company, had an aesthetic sense and appreciated the extreme beauty of the pine forest between the twin lakes, the forest would have been reduced to boards and sawdust long before the turn of the century. But Mr. Buckley insisted on saving this forest of tall pines as long as possible, hoping that someone would eventually purchase the property and preserve the pines and attractive camp sites for people who could fully appreciate them.

Around 1890 a new industry came to the area. The Wylie Cooperage Plant built a sawmill and barrel-making plant on the site of the Indian village on Duck Lake, pushing the Indians out of the area. Along the lake shore and beside the railroad sprang the lumbering village of Wylie, made up of mill workers, their families and suppliers, including the traditional red school house.

Like all sawmills in Michigan, this mill was forced to close when the available supply of suitable timber became exhausted. The mill burned, as did most other sawmills, and the people packed up and moved to other parts, leaving their houses empty—no one would buy them because no one could earn a living there. There was no unemployment insurance then.

About 1900, a young Quaker named Willis Pennington came to Interlochen and was inspired by the forest and lakes. With Frank Gannet of Traverse City, Pennington opened a drug store in Interlochen and began to take an active interest in the community. Pennington foresaw the possibilities of the summer resort business there and made plans to develop it. He purchased land and built a summer hotel on the shore of Green Lake in 1909, appealing to fishermen and hunters for patronage. For awhile his business flourished in summer, and he spent his winters as a drug clerk in Detroit. But fishing became less attractive as highways and railroads opened up the country to the north. The hotel patronage began to wane.

When war broke out in Europe, in 1914, the demand for lumber increased, and the Buckley and Douglas Company decided to cut the pines between the lakes, despite Buckley's protests. To Pennington, the destruction of the pine forest would spell ruin to what remained of his hotel business. With Buckley's help he secured an option on the two hundred acres of land on which grew the great pines. He attempted to form a resort association to promote the area as a vacation place, but our entry into the war frightened prospective investors and the plan had to be abandoned. As a last resort, Pennington went to Lansing and induced the Michigan legislature to purchase the two hundred acres—for the estimated value of the lumber thereon, the land having no real value at that time; now it is valued at as much as $50 per lake-front foot, and there are about eight thousand feet of shoreline.

The area was designated as a public park "to preserve an original pine forest for the people of Michigan and visitors to our state." This was the first state park

Aerial view of the National Music Camp, Interlochen, an example of cultural advancement in the Traverse City area. In the immediate foreground is Kresge Hall.

56

established in Michigan (1917) and the beginning of Michigan's popular system of 73 state parks, to which many millions of visitors come each summer.

The summer hotel business continued to dwindle and Pennington, together with his brother Parker and Parker's wife, pioneered in another activity—the summer camp for girls and boys—which was winning popular approval in the East at that time. Camp Interlochen for girls was opened in 1918 by Mr. and Mrs. Parker Pennington, utilizing the third floor of Hotel Pennington as living quarters. Parents objected to this fire hazard and the Penningtons purchased and moved several of the deserted homes from the ghost town of Wylie to land near the hotel and moved the girls' camp to these buildings. In 1922, Willis Pennington established Camp Penn Loch for boys on the site of the Indian village and the ruins of the Wylie Cooperage Plant on Duck Lake utilizing old lumber sheds and remodeled residences for camp purposes. The little red school house, which served the youth of Wylie during the lumbering days, was moved to a site near the hotel for continued use by the young campers.

In 1926 Willis Pennington read of the spectacular performance at Detroit of the first National High School Orchestra, organized and conducted by Professor Joseph E. Maddy of the University of Michigan. A year later he read of a plan to establish a summer camp—somewhere in Maine—as a training center for this gigantic youth orchestra recruited from all parts of the United States. He immediately contacted Maddy and induced him to consider locating the proposed music camp near Interlochen, where the Hotel Pennington might gain patronage from parents and visitors to this camp.

Maddy was looking for a location where, if possible, the girl members of the orchestra could live on the shore of one lake while the boy members lived on the shore of a different lake nearby, with educational facilities in between. (Coeducational summer camps were unheard of in those days.) The Interlochen location seemed ideal, with an existing girls' camp on one lake and an existing boys' camp on a lake a quarter-mile away, with a spacious hotel and red school house in between. But Maddy and his supporters had no money and no business experience. Some way had to be found to finance such a music camp.

The National High School Orchestra Camp Association (now the National Music Camp) was incorporated in 1927 as a non-profit educational institution by Joseph E. Maddy, Thaddeus P. Giddings and Willis Pennington, with the able assistance of C. M. Tremaine. A contract was entered into by which the Orchestra Camp Association would acquire camp sites adjacent to the existing camps in exchange for the exclusive right to furnish meals to all music campers at an assured rate of profit for a period of five years. This boarding contract was the only possibly way by which such a camp could be established and became the basis for its development during the past thirty-one years into the largest and most famous summer school of the arts in the world. A total number of 3,961 persons from nearly every state and six foreign countries, received one week or more of arts instruction during the 1957 season of the National Music Camp, served by a staff of 635 specialists drawn from the colleges and universities of the nation.

The Days When Wylie Lived

IT WAS late in the nineteenth century when the Wylie Cooperage Company mill was erected in the Interlochen area. The big mill came first and then a score or more of homes for the employees; thus the community of Wylie was born.

The Bill Johnsons ran a boarding house for some of the hands and later put in a stock of staple groceries. Jim Spivle, who still lives at Interlochen, ran a tug which rafted logs across Green Lake and did other work. Rod McLeod was the lake foreman. Hugh Grundy, later electrical inspector for the city of Traverse City, worked for the big mill. Scattered over the community are a number of other former employees who can recall the deep-throated blast of the saw as it bit into giant elm logs.

The company manufactured barrel staves and heads from the elm left standing after the pine had been removed from the area. The big mill, employing about a hundred men, stood on the bank of Green Lake; a set of rails atop a heavily piled pier ran into the lake. Logs were hauled to the pier and dumped into the water where they were rafted and boomed ready for the saw.

The old "trestle," as the pier was called, held seven loads of logs at one time. The pier was twenty-two feet above the surface of the lake, the height of railway and cars added another eight feet. This height is cited to illustrate one of the "toughest man" stories ever to come out of the woods. It was in the winter of 1902 or 1903 that a little Irishman named Jim White was working atop a car load of pine. He slipped and fell the thirty feet to the frozen surface of the lake, landing on his head and shoulders. Jim walked home and suffered nothing more than a little headache.

Wages for the Wylie Cooperage Company hands started at 40 cents a day for ten hours, scaling upward to $60.00 per month and found. This wage was for skilled office men and similar categories. Hugh Grundy related how he worked up through the various jobs to that of bookkeeper. He was almost everything but tailsawyer and headsawyer. At one time he was engineer on the *Old Betsie*, the tug which plied the waters of the lake.

Traverse City was the heart of the region in that day, much as it is today. Wylie was located fifteen miles away and its men from the woods got into town only two or three times a year. Supplies were brought by rail and employees invented their own play.

A few ruins and a lot of memories are about all that remain of Wylie. On the same site the sound of the tuba and violin have replaced the music of the mill whistle and the saw. Where the storage sheds stood for the cooperage firm there now stand two new cabins for the National Music Camp. Peter Hendges piled lumber and staves on the exact spot where he later built the cabins. Still jutting into the lake are the giant piles which supported the dock, and on the shore a couple of rotting hardwood logs still can be seen, washed by the waves of the years.

Before the days of the Wylie Cooperage Company, giant virgin pine logs were cut and piled along the banks of the Little Betsie River and along the shores of Green Lake. Came the spring break-up, the dam at the old Thompson mill was blasted out and countless thousands of feet of timber moved down the Little Betsie, across Green Lake, and then down the Big Betsie to Frankfort where the L. W. Crain Company bought them.

For the drive, Mrs. Mary Leatherland operated a boarding house. She had a cook shack and eating hall built on a wannigan of white pine and with it made the trip to Frankfort with the men. That is, until her daughter, Bernice, fell off the raft one day and came near drowning. From that time on she refused to ride the wannigan. Bernice Leatherland is now eighty years old and her recollections of these times are still sharp. Known in the Interlochen community by her married name, Bernice Conrad, she came to the community when she was one-and-a-half years old.

What became of Wylie? Much of the old property is now owned by the National Music Camp and only a couple of the original buildings remain. One building was once the home of Pete Fisher, superintendent for the company; it is abandoned and in ruins.

The Acme Woolen Mill

"ANNOUNCEMENT was made here this morning that the new Scripture and Hoxie Woolen Mill, Acme, will be open for business within the near future.

"The company, a partnership between John Scripture and John Hoxie, will accept good clear fleeces for carding and preparation for spinning and weaving. A premium price is being paid for long staple Lincoln wool and for the finer grades of Merino wool.

"As soon as production is under way at the mill, a system of exchange will be established whereby local owners of herds will be able to exchange their raw wool for the finished woolen material.

"Because of the high standards being set for the mill, Mr. Scripture and Mr. Hoxie have both stated that only the finest wool will be acceptable for the looms and tag material or black fleeces will not be purchased."

The above could well have been a story taken from the Traverse City paper late in the nineteenth century. It was about fifty-eight years ago that the mill was established and opened for business. Located just west of the present highway through the village were two dams that supplied water to the mill, says John Newcomb.

Located on the banks of Acme Creek, the mill was an addition to an old sawmill already in operation; it was powered by a low head of water held by twin dams. It was a three-story structure and was painted a bright red. Five looms were operated on the first floor to turn out the very finest grades of material, woven, in most part, from fleeces bought locally.

Carding was done on the third floor, and the stairways were always slippery with the oil from the wool. Wool fat was not a merchantable product in those early days since it was not until recently that it was purified and refined sufficiently to appear on the markets under fancy trade names for shampoo and hand lotion.

Mrs. John Newcomb, a resident of Traverse City, was one of the weavers in the old mill. She helped produce the fine checks, plaids and worsteds which won considerable recognition over the northern part of the state.

A survey of the old mill site reveals only a few rotted timbers and a scattering of crumbling masonry.

In addition to the woolen mill, the Hoxie family operated a sawmill which did a flourishing business during the early days. The pond which provided the water power also furnished a backwater for floating logs.

Shortly after the establishment of the Scripture and Hoxie mill, a second woolen mill was established in Acme. This one was organized by Henry Buller. His initial investment was secured, apparently, by a mortgage on the Robert Buller farm and on the mill property. After a short operation he closed his mill and moved to Traverse City, starting a new mill on Front Street, West. Whether the mill operated profitably after that, or not, is not known. The thread of information ends at that point.

The Scripture and Hoxie mill at Acme, however, the original one, continued to produce fine materials for four years or more. Just why it suspended operation is not a matter of record. One version is that woolen materials could be imported from downstate and from the Middle West at a lower cost than they could be manufactured locally.

The "grist" system established by Scripture and Hoxie was, as far as records go, successful. A farmer could shear his sheep in the spring and take a couple of hundred pounds of wool to the mill. There it would be weighed with tare deducted. A percentage of the original weight would then be returned to the raiser in finished woolen cloth. John Newcomb explained that the finished material was of unusually high quality and a suit which he purchased "nearly outwore me."

A tailor service was maintained at the mill through a portion of its existence and, while the tailoring would not be considered top quality by modern standards, the tailor sewed a firm seam and his coats and trousers wore on and on. Blankets woven at Acme were until recent years in use at the Traverse City State Hospital.

Materials for ladies' skirts were also woven on the Acme looms. There are still recollections among the local feminine population of fancy plaids and plain colors in lightweight cloth.

With Acme again growing rapidly and setting a fast pace for other up-and-coming villages, there should be little wonder if a similar plant someday opened within its limits.

Williamsburg

MILL CREEK wasn't much of a settlement at first. There were three families from Monroe County, New York, who arrived in 1856. Then came the Langworthy, Button, Brown, Odell and a half dozen other hardy families. That was the beginning of Williamsburg, a rural town which changed its location but never its outlook on the future. Just when the name "Mill Creek" was dropped and the name "Williamsburg" accepted is not actually known. It was, however, before the establishment of a postoffice. Mill Creek was a fast stream of water which now crosses M-72 a few rods east of the present village. The old town was located on the creek about a quarter of a mile south. Not until the railroad was established, and the road built, did the town move to its present site.

This story is about two of the hardiest of the early arrivals, Kossuth Stites and A. W. Eaton.

After the Civil War the Williamsburg community took on added bustle and activity. The old Truman Scofield grist and sawmill was furnishing considerable employment for the residents and the land was very productive for farming. Scofield's mill needed a manager in 1878 and A. W. Eaton arrived to take over the job. He was a skillful operator and the mill turned out more grist and cut more board feet of lumber than ever before. The village prospered.

One of the best men in the mill at that time was Kossuth Stites. He could file a big saw, scale a load of logs, cruise a piece of timber or do any of the other jobs associated with lumbering.

Eaton and Stites looked the lumber situation over carefully and decided there was room for another mill in Williamsburg. Just like that. They talked it over with David Vinton, another resident of the community, and he decided to

64

venture with the men. He was never an active partner in the Eaton and Stites mill but he did put up an undisclosed sum of money.

The mill machinery was shipped from Kalamazoo by rail to Traverse City and then brought the rest of the way by team. The site chosen for the new saw-mill was just beyond the present village of Williamsburg and on the south side of M-72. A close look today will show a beautiful flowing well, which was drilled when the mill was built about seventy-five years ago. The well furnished water for the big boilers and has never stopped flowing.

The railroad cut through just south of the mill. It was constructed on a trestle so teams and loads of logs could get through under the tracks. It was later graded as it is today.

Lumber from the saws was piled east of the mill and, as was the custom in those days, the slabs were fired. There is no record of the number of thousands of feet of lumber cut by the Eaton and Stites mill. What is known is that the two pioneers set a pattern of prosperity in the community that has never been removed.

The death of A. W. Eaton in 1888 ended the profitable partnership. The mill was purchased by Dave Vinton and one of his sons and Kossuth Stites, who remained on as superintendent. Later it was sold to Albert DeVries. It operated until 1904 when, late in the year, it was torn down. This final chapter in the lumbering history of Williamsburg was supervised by Kossuth Stites. He stood by to direct the destruction of the mill which he had helped build.

To the old ones of the community the "new" Williamsburg is a passing fancy. To them there will never be any Williamsburg other than the one which was build around the Scofield mill and, more emphatically, around the Eaton and Stites mill. Old Williamsburg, before the coming of the rails, was no boom town. There were two general stores, a drug store, hotel, postoffice, creamery and a lot of nice homes. The homes are still there back from the highway, but the business block is gone these many years. Only the steps remain of the old I.O.O.F. Hall. The Vinton Hotel was recently a mission house. The drug store and the two general stores have been torn down. The main street was known as "the Square," and where it meets M-72 was "Creamery Corners" because, as you would suppose, there was a creamery there.

The town hall, built in 1889, stands, and the Methodist Church, built in 1881, is still in a fine state of repair. The old dam continues to hold a head of water and spills over the cement raceway. Old millstones lie on the bank of the pond, and the Scofield mill property, now owned by Dr. B. B. Bushong, is being kept in excellent condition.

The roar of the water from the dam and the steady jet from the artesian well on the Eaton and Stites site, are monuments to a hardy people of a century past.

A typical hardwood lumbering camp. Some camps were more pretentious, but many consisted only of two or three buildings to house the lumberjacks.

Mable Didn't Grow Up

THERE was every reason to believe that some day Mable would be a "big girl." But the lumbering industry waned and Mable died. That is the story, in a few words, of the village of Mable, which flourished, floundered and faded at the end of the last century and the beginning of the present one.

Mable, named for the daughter of Thomas T. Bates, pioneer publisher, was located east of the present village of Williamsburg where M-72 turns left. A dirt road extends eastward through the old site of the village.

Originally, the site of the village was a forty-acre farm owned by George Humphrey. The land was covered by a heavy stand of hard maple trees and was operated as a sugarbush for many years.

A portable sawmill, owned by Warren Hastings, moved into the area about 1893 and with it the first commercial building. The store building later became the postoffice, which was established when the railroad came. The rails cut diagonally across the old Humphrey farm.

James Button, who was born on the site of the old village, recalled vividly his youth and the hardships of that time: "There was a stage from Barker Creek to Acme and we could either walk to Williamsburg for our mail or go to Barker Creek. Then Charlie Eaton took over the mail route and we had better service."

With the coming of the rails and regular postal service, a sidetrack was built. Logs, ties, lumber, poles and potatoes were shipped from Mable in vast quantities.

Though the first working sawmill was erected by Hastings, there had been an earlier mill which had not been too successful. Button had decided to do a little mill work by utilizing the power of a tiny creek which flows across the present site of M-72, but he was unfamiliar with mill construction or engineering

67

and was not a great success. After his mill structure was completed he discovered that there was not sufficient power to operate it, so he dug a channel from a nearby creek to get additional power. However, this was not found to be practical. The earthworks of this mill are still to be seen near the railroad grade; the ditch which was made to run the two small streams together is also still in evidence.

Highlight in the life of Mable came when the newspapers of the Middle West carried a single paragraph story of the drilling of an unusual well near Gilbert Pray's general store. That was in 1908. The well, still flowing a steady stream, is seventy feet deep and, at the time it was first drilled, had a forty-five foot waterhead. Water from the first flow shot into the air higher than the store and the flow was estimated at 202,677 gallons a day, enough to supply the needs of a village of four thousand persons. At that time it was believed to be one of the largest water flows in Michigan. The well was driven by the Gardner and Son Company.

Descendants of the pioneer families are still living in the region. Such names as Pray, Gilbert, Hastings, Fairbanks, Button, Wilkinson, and many more are the backbone of that and the surrounding country. An unusual item of interest is that the people who still live at the site of the village always refer to their place of residence as Mable, even though the town has gone and the postoffice has been closed these many years.

Fife Lake

IN THE beginning there were two villages: Northtown and Southtown. To the few residents they were known as North Fife Lake and Fyfe Lake, Grand Traverse County. Fyfe Lake was platted in June of 1872 by J. L. Shaw and a group of associates from Grand Rapids. The plat was in the interest of the Grand Rapids and Indiana Railroad which was extending its rails northward to tap the rich pine and hardwood area of the region. North Fife Lake was platted at the same time by Thomas T. Bates, who had purchased the property from Morgan Bates.

There has been a lot of discussion about the name of Fife Lake and why there is so much confusion regarding its correct spelling. Actually the railroad officials made an error when they spelled it Fyfe Lake. The village was named for the lake on the shores of which it was built. The lake, prior to the platting, had been named for William H. Fife, of Acme, a highway commissioner, who accompanied a survey party into the area in 1867 which had been ordered to survey the ground for a road from Traverse City to Houghton Lake.

The highway was to be built as a state road from non-resident money. The survey was to provide for a "Y" at Fife Lake with one branch going to Midland and the other hitting Grand Traverse Bay at a point where Acme is now located. The road was never completed. In fact, the surveyors couldn't even complete the survey because of difficulty they encountered in getting supplies. The state Supreme Court ruled the financing program unconstitutional, and that was as far as the project went.

Anyway, that was the beginning of Fife Lake.

With two towns platted in a roaring lumbering country, it was natural that friction would arise between the residents of the respective settlements. An example of the suspicion with which the two settlements regarded each other is found in the argument about the location of the original depot for the Grand Rapids and Indiana Railroad. The first location was in Northtown, now Fife Lake proper. There was a bitter fight about this site, and the depot was in operation only a short time when it burned down. How the fire started no one knew. The next depot was built in Southtown and, as a resident of the days said, "at an inconvenient distance from the principal business center."

One of the early business places in Southtown was a general store owned by John S. Schoonover. The store building still stands on what was the main street of the village; the Schoonover sign is still readable on one side of the weathered structure.

The original plats of the two towns covered about sixty acres, but there was a common belief that the upper plat would be the most quickly developed. Tracy and Thurber built a hotel on the hill overlooking the lake and the Thompson brothers built a mill to begin cutting lumber into boards. The building of the hotel was held up for some time awaiting the first boards to come from the saws.

The first log went to the saw in August 1872, and produced six hundred feet of lumber. It took thirty minutes to reduce the large pine log to boards.

In June 1872, a man named J. B. Lancaster opened a small store in a shack on what was then the state road, originally surveyed in 1867.

In 1880, the two villages, referred to as "Uppertown" and "Lowertown," took on the air of a metropolis. Their population was nearly one thousand people. A report made shortly before that date showed that there were nine saloons and only two church organizations.

Fife Lake today is much the same as it was in 1880 as far as the old buildings are concerned. The old LaBar Drug Store and liquor store is still occupied by a similar business, now operated by Frank Hostman. The old records show beverage tax license papers dating as far back as 1893. Of course, the old tax licenses permitted the holder to sell whiskey by the barrel instead of by the pint. Hostman also has an old opium permit issued to the store as well as a tobacco sales license.

Some of the families which helped make history in the Fife Lake area were the Petersons, the Fosters, the Rancours, the Campbells, and the Andersons.

70

The number of the real pioneers of the village, however, can be counted on your fingers. In 1875 there were John Johnson, the shoemaker; James Hodges, Sr., Solomon Mills, John Cane, Robert Pierce, Elias Benton, and James Ward.

A Peterson opened a blacksmith shop in 1878. He made wagons and carriages as well as doing routine smithy work.

David Rancour, one of the older pioneers and lumberjacks of the area, remembers the old state road before it was moved to the present location. He can point out the first grave in the old cemetery and explain why it is at the very back of the dedicated plot. When May Gibson died she was buried in the first lot nearest the main highway. Then the road was resurveyed and it passed the cemetery on the opposite side. Traces of the old highway can still be seen north of the village.

One of the big sawmills was built by Chickering and Kysor. They built the mill in 1881 and, the year following, built a planing mill. Capacity of the mill was fifty thousand feet of pine per day.

Early supremacy of the Uppertown was believed assured when a postoffice was approved. H. B. Thurber was named postmaster. He was succeeded by a man named Billings, who immediately thereafter moved away from the village and was never approved by the Postoffice Department. James Montieth was next named to the job and, soon after, the postoffice was moved to the north village.

Gradually the advantages of the lower plat became apparent and more and more business and industry concentrated there. It was more convenient to the railway and there was no hill to climb.

To compare the village of Fife Lake today with the settlement of 1882 requires a lot of imagination. In that day there were five general stores, four hotels, three hat and millinery stores, three shoe shops and a score of other business places.

During its life the village has had three weekly newspapers. First there was the *Fife Lake Eye*, which suspended operations after financial difficulties in its first year of operation. It was followed by the *Fife Lake Comet*, which had a longer and more successful life. The last was the *Fife Lake Monitor*, which was published until shortly before World War I.

Today, the town is a resort center. Rarely is there an available piece of property around the beautiful lake. Cottage and home owners from all over the

Midwest know the town as a fine place to vacation, away from summer heat and the hectic bustle of the cities.

Located just east of U.S. Route 131, the town and its environs afford a quiet country atmosphere, pleasant people and an historical background which reeks with lore and legend.

Typical of the spirit which prevailed when "old maid Andrews" ran her picture studio and made hair watch-chains for her patrons, is this remark, made by a present resident of the village: "There's nothing wrong with anyone in Fife Lake that Indian 'yarbs,' leaves and roots won't cure."

Walton Junction Lived It Up!

WALTON JUNCTION, in the southern part of Grand Traverse County, began with the arrival of the Grand Rapids and Indiana Railway early in 1873. Within a few years the village was known from one end of the railway district to the other as Hell. A lumberjack could go into the ticket office in South Bend, Indiana, and ask for a ticket to Hell, and the agent would turn around to the slotted rack, take out a Walton one-way, and hand it through the wicket.

But this was dubious fame. It was born of the fact that the village had the misfortune to be located between Cadillac and Traverse City and thus was a stopping-off point for rivermen, lumberjacks and the hangers-on of the lumber camps.

The first business in the village was a boarding house built by A. F. Phillip, who came to the area as foreman of a gang of railroad workers. After the completion of the road he remained with the railroad as a foreman for about two years and then went into the hotel business. He operated the boarding house for several years and later built and operated the Grand Rapids and Indiana House, another boarding place.

Lumber camps of all kinds dotted the area around the village, and the semblance of a settlement caused a number of businessmen to take an interest in the possibilities of locating there.

The Stronach Lumber Company established a supply depot there. In 1878, Hannah, Lay and Company, Traverse City, bought their interests and in addition to their supply station, set up a general mercantile business.

The first road from Traverse City which extended to the Manistee River was opened by H. A. Ferris, a land-looker, who arrived in the region in 1870.

73

In 1880 he built a saloon in Walton, considering it a lively enough place in which to sell his wares.

A third "hotel" was opened in 1875 when Robert Knaggs built the Walton House. This was later named the Exchange and, sometime later, burned to the ground.

The fame (or notoriety) of Walton arose from the keen and sometimes brutal rivalry between lumberjacks and crews of the different camps. Cadillac men, after a few nips of barrel whiskey, would head for Walton, where they knew they would have very little difficulty getting accommodated with a fight because the jacks from Traverse City were usually there with the same idea.

One of the classic battles took place at Cedar Creek, now Manton. This was in or about the year of 1882 when Clam Lake, now Cadillac, was bending every effort to move the county seat from Cedar Creek. Residents of Clam Lake felt that their location was more central and would be better for all concerned. Cedar Creekers had an act of the legislature to back them in that it designated that the seat should be near the bridge across the Manistee River.

Somehow, word got around that the Clam Lake bully boys were heading for Cedar Creek in an effort to settle the affair for all time. Word was spread along the rails to Walton and Traverse City, and a large crew met the Clam Lake boys when they arrived at Cedar Creek.

The fight which followed was a campfire tale for half a century and is still, today, told by some of the older lumberjacks. The boys from the south were beaten back, and one lumberjack from Traverse City returned home with one ear in a paper sack. He wanted a local doctor to see if it could be stitched back in place.

There was bad blood, too, between the woods crews and the rivermen. The location of Walton between the Big Manistee and the Boardman rivers made it handy for hundreds of the men to get together for a "friendly fight" on weekends.

John Anderson, who was a railroad brakeman in Traverse City for many years, knew and met many of the boys from the camps. He recalled one fight in Fife Lake (just a short distance from Walton Junction) in which two of the top jacks fought for an hour. When it was all over they spent a week in the Traverse City Hospital getting ready for another scrap.

Mark Craw, an officer in this region for the Conservation Department, a fledging organization in 1900, had his troubles with the Waltonians, too. At this time a group of enterprising men from Illinois decided that there was money to be made in cranberries. Walton had a good stream of water running through a bog area and there was a small lake for a backwater. Turning thoughts into deeds, they brought crews to the village and trenched several acres of the bog. The project prospered for several years and brought scores of Indian berry harvesters to the area.

The cranberry growers' bane was muskrats, which constantly dug tunnels under the ridges and caved them in. They appealed to the Conservation Department to permit trapping of the animals. They got permission to do so, provided the pelts were turned in to the authorities. They caught the rats but failed to bring in the pelts. Officer Craw spent many long days trying to enforce the proviso. His trouble ended when the cranberry business faded away. The bog and a scattering of plants are still there showing where the enterprise existed, the only one in Walton other than the sawmills.

Along the Grand Rapids and Indiana rails at Walton there mushroomed several business buildings. One was the depot; another was the Ellis Saloon; a third, the Phillips Saloon, which George McManus later ran for many years. McManus sold barrel liquor and sold it for one purpose: to drink. If the drink caused a fight that was none of his concern.

He had a close friend, called by many his bodyguard, by the name of Flip Gillispi. Flip was a little, dark-skinned, quiet-mannered person who never went out of his way to find trouble—or avoid it, either. He always carried an old frontier-type six-shooter and got his name from his favorite trick of flipping a coin into the air and shooting it with his revolver. One incident involving him bears recording. There was a friendly poker game in progress in the Ellis Saloon, with a considerable stake on the table. An argument arose over who had won it. Gillispi was one of the players. Another was a burley toploader named Black Jack. Gillispi closed the argument abruptly by pulling out his six-shooter and putting a hole through the ceiling of the saloon. Black Jack pushed the pot across the table: "You've got the best hand, Flip," he said.

No one remembers what became of Flip.

The McManus Saloon, run for a time by Jack Witkop, still stands. It has been turned around to face the road and was, for a time, used to accommodate hunters. It is the only remaining original business building.

Besides claiming credit for being the roughest, toughest town in the state, Walton had another small claim to immortality. Some of the cleverest riverhogs in the country worked near the village.

One of the best was Harvey Collins. He was a foreman over a crew of jam runners. He could birl a log with the best and never get wet. An example of his talents was demonstrated one day when he had a few drinks. He picked up an empty kerosene barrel and tossed it in the Manistee and then proceeded to birl it—end over end.

Then there was the Indian chap named Ferguson. His favorite trick was to ride a peeled cedar post down the middle of the Manistee River and then birl it to shore.

Some of the bully boys in the Walton area also live in tales of the lumbering era. In addition to George McManus, who was an artist with his fists, there were several others. One of the McManus episodes which has lived was a minor argument with a fellow named Frank DeGray, a riverhog. The argument was settled very quietly when McManus slapped DeGray with the flat of his hand and rendered him unconscious for more than half an hour.

Jacobs was another character. On the slightest provocation, he would down a double shot of bar whiskey, flop over on his hands and walk on his hands the distance of two city blocks, despite his 225 pounds.

Walton Junction died when the pine and hardwood disappeared and the mills ceased to run. The schoolhouse has been torn down and only the cement base remains. The foundation of the water tower, which furnished water for the railroad engines, is also still there, and a couple of the early residential places remain.

Memories of the village lie in the little cemetery in the woods. The main highway has bypassed the place, and Walton Junction is a name only. The scars of its ribald days are gone and the pain of its bruises forgotten.

PLEASANT VILLAGES, BEAUTIFUL CHURCHES

Previous to the year 1847, there was not a white man living in all Leelanau County. From Cat Head Point to the present boundary of Benzie County, it was an unbroken forest, inhabited almost entirely by wild beasts.

Crystal Lake Channel

DURING the second week of August 1873, a house and office building was erected on a scow near the village of Frankfort in Benzie County, and thus began one of the most important engineering projects ever, until that time, to be undertaken in northern Michigan. It was the dredging and clearing of the Betsie River, the clearing of a strip of land from the Betsie River to Crystal Lake, and the opening of the lake to steamer passage to the Great Lakes.

The project was conceived in the minds of a number of residents and property owners in the Crystal Lake and Frankfort area. Almost countless thousands of feet of timber were unavailable for milling because of the lack of transportation. The opening of the new waterway would make them available.

Ringleader in the canal promotion was Archibald Jones, a fruit farmer who had moved to the Benzie County community from Merengo, Illinois. He was perhaps sixty-five or seventy years old at the time but had the energy of a man half his age.

First step in the operation was the organization of the Navigation Company of the County of Benzie. Mention of this fledging company was made in the *Benzie Journal* and later in the *Grand Traverse Herald* of July 17, 1873; the organization was also sometimes referred to as the Betsie River Improvement Company.

Stock in the new organization was sold at $25.00 a share and there were a lot of takers at the beginning.

On August 14, 1873, the *Grand Traverse Herald* again carried a piece about the project. The story pointed out that enthusiasm was high and that the people were determined to make a success of the enterprise.

Now, it should be mentioned that a semblance of a survey was made to determine if the plan was feasible. Who made this survey is not known, and it is very likely that he left the Frankfort-Benzonia community the same year he made known his findings. The report assured the backers of the canal that the water of Crystal Lake was approximately four-and-a-half feet above the surface of Lake Michigan. The lowering of Crystal Lake would provide a nice beach which the body of water did not, at that time, have, and would establish a new water route to the big lake and make a lot of money for everyone.

Leland, in 1880, the county seat of Leelanau County. It was once an important producer of pig iron and charcoal as is indicated by the eight kilns pictured here.

In reviewing the situation, and to get a proper picture of the lake which the company proposed to lower, one must visualize a beautiful body of water with no beaches. Hills on all sides of the lake made it impossible to even walk on a strip of beach without getting into the water.

Where the village of Beulah now stands there was deep water, deep enough for shallow draft boats to pull right up to the foot of what is now the site of the Benzie County courthouse. Where there wasn't water there was a quagmire of bog and rushes. The present site of the Northway Hotel was under water. The site of the first house built in Beulah, the residence of Attorney M. G. Paul, was deep beneath the surface of Crystal Lake.

Concerning the particular point where the Paul home is located there is a

79

story of an Indian youth whose sweetheart accidently drowned at the foot of the steep hill now known as Lookout or Lover's Leap. The young Indian then threw himself from the hill directly into the water and was drowned apparently in hope that he would be with his sweetheart in death.

Second step in opening the lake was the clearing of the Betsie River to make it deep enough for the unobstructed flow of boat traffic. This was started with the afore mentioned construction of the scow and residence office which headed upstream from Frankfort.

On August 21, 1873, the *Grand Traverse Herald* stated that the work was started "last Wednesday noon," and that by the end of the week the crew and the little scow had progressed to "the landing." A blast on the scow whistle on the following Monday signaled the continuance of the work, and by Tuesday evening the scow had reached Perry's mill. The newspaper account further states that the operation would have its work completed to the state road bridge by the following Wednesday evening. Workmen hoped to reach the point where the proposed channel would be cut through a week later.

The channel was staked off from the south side of the lake, just north of the present county farm. The distance of swamp and wilderness to be cut through was about a mile, and the doughty Archibald Jones felt that a small cut to let the water out of the lake would be sufficient since the natural rush of the current would do the dredging.

Another piece in a Traverse City newspaper pointed out that actual work on the clearing of the channel right-of-way began in August. This was about August 15, 1873. The land was cleared to a width of a hundred feet and the proposed canal would be thirty feet wide.

Then the inevitable happened. There was a lack of funds. The residents of the community had failed to subscribe for the full amount of stock and there was still $7,000 worth of shares unsold on September 4, 1873. The *Benzie Journal* explained that many of the people who would benefit the most were contributing the least. In response to an appeal, a number of individuals pledged labor in lieu of money, working out the value of the pledges at $1.25 a day.

During the first week of September, 1873, a crew of workmen began to remove the ridge of earth which held back the water of Crystal Lake. Their work was not unlike laying the cornerstone for a new monument to prosperity, the unveiling of a new era of progress. Chronicled at the time, a newspaper account of the opening stated "the waters of the lake rushed out in great violence. The soil of the swamp through which the outlet passes being soft and porous, the rushing waters wore it rapidly away. At the time of our report the channel was wide and deep and the lake had been lowered four feet. It is believed that a level of at least eight feet below the surface of the lake will be reached. The new beach is dry, clean, and hard enough for a race course."

On Thursday, September 25, the water was still rushing out of Crystal Lake and a joint stock company had already been organized to build a hotel on the new beach. Another newspaper mention was made on December 18, 1873. The shoreline timber that had been worthless before the canal was dug was selling for $9.00 a thousand. But, if that was a benefit, there was widespread disappointment in the results obtained by the canal.

Residents of Benzonia envisioned steamers plying their trade around the silver beach of the lake. They saw a great new empire growing as the result of the easy access to the Great Lakes.

But the nearest the good people ever came to realization of their dream was when the little steamer *Onward* left port at Frankfort and headed for Crystal Lake on the crest of the flood. Captain Chris Miller was at the wheel and Bob Blacklock was the engineer on the Sunday morning the trip was made.

Miller must have been a master, for he negotiated the roaring current and rounded Crystal Lake with his steam whistle blaring at every turn. The *Onward* picked up a few passengers along the circuit of the lake and returned to Frankfort. She was the only steamer ever to negotiate the entire round trip.

In the meantime the Navigation Company of the County of Benzie had let a contract for a specially constructed boat to be put in operation on the channel and on the newly cleared Betsie River. The boat was built in Manistee by John Torrence. It was designed with a flat bottom and was paddlewheel propelled. The boat was twelve feet of beam and forty feet long. During the early summer in 1874 the squat little craft made her maiden voyage down the new canal and the Betsie. It was a nightmare of a trip and the craft made it stern first most of the way so her heavy paddles could cut through sand bars and mud flats. She never returned to Crystal Lake. For a while she did duty in the Frankfort harbor, towing rafts. She was never christened but was called the "Mudhen" by the folks of the region. She ended her days as a Mississippi River boat, where she proved her worth as a speedy and capable craft.

There was litigation as a result of the boat building venture. It was over a matter of an unpaid balance for her building and machinery. When the venerable Archibald Jones was hauled into court to answer why the boat would not navigate he advised the august court in this manner:

"If you want to know why the boat wouldn't float I may say that it was because the bottom of the river was too close to the top of the water."

The story of the fiasco did not end there. The lake level—which had gone down too low—had to be raised, and there was a problem in engineering even greater than the original one. Stopping up the gap in the south side of the lake where the waters had rushed out was no easy matter. Several efforts were made before the citizens called in William Joyce of Thompsonville. This was several years after the canal had been dug. Joyce felled trees across the gap, piled tons of brush on and added fill dirt until a dam was created. Later a cement structure with a fish weir was installed.

The channel and the Betsie River provided a waterway for the rafting of logs to the mills and to the blast furnace at Frankfort but there was constant bickering and litigation among the lumbermen in regard to it. Even today, there remains a quantity of submerged timber in the Betsie and the deadhead rights are likely to be used in reclamation.

Brundage Settlement

IT WAS a newly erected white cross over a grave far from the beaten path that attracted the bird hunter. The unidentified hunter could not recall having seen the grave before and he had hunted the area many times. He did the logical thing and notified authorities. A federal man and an officer from the Benzie County sheriff's department investigated and found that the grave, that of a little boy, was at least fifty years old and was a part of the old Brundage settlement in Inland Township near Honor. It seems a mother, Mrs. Robert Mitchell, had remembered her dead son and had planted a rosebush and erected the new marker. This was in 1956.

The Brundage Cemetery has only a half dozen graves, all but one occupied by members of the pioneer Brundage family. The one grave, unmarked, is that of a lumberjack whose identity has long since been forgotten.

B. C. Brundage pre-empted the land more than eighty years ago. It was high ground and was heavily timbered. From the forest he hewed a place to build a home and later cleared a goodly portion of the land for farming. He planted an orchard and the future looked bright.

But one can't constantly take from the soil without returning some substance, and the light land soon became exhausted. In those few words is the story of the Brundage farm.

Yet, in the years that B. C. Brundage lived the area became sufficiently settled to establish a school district with as many as twenty-five students. A cemetery was platted and dedicated. First buried was Emeline Brundage, who died on May 4, 1874. She was the daughter of B. C. Brundage and was buried on the extreme west side of the cemetery. The marker over her grave is weathered and broken and the entire area is overgrown with sumac and brambles.

Ira Case, at eighty-four years of age, remembered the Brundage farm well. In fact, he married one of the school teachers, Edith Collison, who served the Brundage district. Another oldtimer who remembered the Brundage family well was Jud Andrus. Jud was a student in the old school and tramped two miles morning and night to and from classes.

The old schoolhouse was torn down nearly a half century ago. The farm home and big barn and the out-buildings were weathered and wracked by time. Later, they, too, fell apart and were torn down, the lumber and timbers being used in miscellaneous construction around the area. The land eventually reverted to the state.

Today, there is only the old cemetery with its tall grass, gnarled sumac, briars, and scrub oak and an ancient apple orchard to mark the site. Deer wander into the place and munch apples which themselves date the planting. There are russets, northern spies, talman sweets and snow apples, all favorites of a half century ago. The cemetery is the property of Inland Township and there is some talk in the community of cleaning it up and making it a credit to the pioneers who lived, worked and died in the loneliness of the northern wilderness.

The name of the family will live on, however, for a swift brook of cold water courses through a valley only a few rods from the old Brundage home. It is appropriately called Brundage Creek.

Lake Ann Still Lives

Lake Ann, July 4, 1897.—This town is a mass of smouldering ruins, and there are scarcely a dozen buildings left standing. The entire business portion of the village has been swept clean by the most disastrous conflagration that has ever visited this locality.

THAT WAS the way the *Grand Traverse Herald*, Traverse City's weekly newspaper, described the fire which swept Lake Ann village, on Lake Ann, Benzie County, when it was at its heyday and had dreams of outstripping Traverse City as a metropolis.

It was a pleasant day, July 3, 1897. A stiff southeast wind was blowing and the community was, almost to a man, making preparations for a celebration of the Fourth. A majority of the people were planning to go to Thompsonville or to Manistee for the occasion, and many of them had already departed to spend the holiday with friends or relatives or to get an early start with their picnics, fireworks and fun.

William Habbler's big sawmill on the shore of Lake Ann was idle, and the tug, which was also owned by Habbler, was moored near the shore. It was one-thirty in the afternoon and a faint wisp of smoke came from the big mill stack and disappeared in the wind.

No one knows whether a spark from the anchored tug, or one from the boiler fire in the engine room of the mill, started the flames.

Irv Youmans, about ten years old at the time, lived with his parents on a hill at the edge of the village. The hill, known as Gopher Heights, overlooked the entire business district and the big Habbler mill. He was the first to see the flames as they began to leap from the mill on the shore. Irv raced to the Putnam and Burnett General Store on the main corners, gave the alarm and then ran to give the alarm at the Habbler store, which was directly in the path of the flames. The wind was blowing from the southeast and had increased to near gale velocity. Acres of heading material—thousands of feet of lumber and mountains of slabs and sawdust—surrounded the big Habbler mill, and it was only a matter of minutes before the flames were roaring skyward in one of the greatest fires the region has ever known.

The fire fighting equipment at the mill was called into play but was found inadequate and useless. The village water supply was exhausted almost immediately. It came from a large wooden tank atop a hill just outside the village, near Gopher Heights. A water ram in Ransom Creek forced the water into the tank to provide the reserve. However, when an emergency arose, the ram was found incapable of operating with sufficient volume to meet the need.

An emergency call was telegraphed by N. E. Degan, Manistee and Northeastern Railway agent, to Traverse City and the bell atop the Union Street Fire Station was rung for volunteers. Twenty men responded, headed by Acting Fire Chief J. W. Fulghum and assisted by J. W. Milliken. The horse-drawn steamer was hauled to the railroad depot on north Union Street and loaded onto a flatcar. Engineer John Halter backed Engine Number Four onto the car and William Higgins, the conductor, dropped the coupling pin. Fireman George Halter fed fuel to the boiler and the firemen made the first eight miles in six minutes. Then the flat car developed a hotbox and the pace was slowed by two stops to pour water on a heated axle.

Yet, fifty-four minutes after the alarm was received in Traverse City, the men were pouring two streams of water on the flaming village. Hose lines were stretched over piles of slabs and sawdust and around smoking ruins as water was pumped from Lake Ann into the center of the holocaust. Women who weren't busy with the saving of their own personal property served black coffee to the weary firemen.

To the Traverse City Department went the credit for saving the Habbler hoop factory (not the cooperage), a portion of the piled lumber and a few buildings.

Soon after the fire started, it became evident to the residents of the village that little could be done to save their homes and business places, and every able-bodied person not manning fire equipment was pressed into service removing household goods to safety.

The Park Hotel, located across from the Habbler store, was filled with drummers and regular guests. Their trunks and personal belongings were stacked around a bandstand which stood in the little park in the center of the village, where they and other property were burned to ashes, while the ornate bandstand was left untouched.

Flames roared upward with such force that flaming cooperage lumber was hurtled skyward as far as the eye could see. Houses a half mile from the village were struck and burned.

There was tragedy, too. A Mrs. Masters, age eighty, mother of Mrs. Harry Baker, had been removed to a point of safety across the railroad right of way to the west. On her person she carried some important papers she had grabbed from her burning house which was located across the road east of the E. C. Lake home. However, after reaching the distant spot of safety, she remembered some cherished pillow slips and returned to get them. The home was by this time all aflame, and immediately after she entered the house the walls collapsed, and she died in the holocaust.

The story of the fire—the tragic loss to the people of the village and the generosity accorded the destitute residents by the surrounding area—is one that went on record as a day to be remembered by the pioneer residents of the village.

William Habbler suffered the greatest loss. His big mill on the shore of the lake, his general store and its large stock of goods, his home and his cooperage plant, all were destroyed. On the entire property he carried a total of $5,500 in insurance, the largest amount carried in the village. In fact, there was only a total of about $10,000 of insurance on the entire loss with many of the business places and homes without a cent of insurance protection.

Martin Stack owned the only saloon in the village. Located in a small frame building just north of the Putnam and Burnett General Store, it was one of the first buildings to go. For several weeks following the fire he remained undecided whether or not to rebuild. He finally reopened for business in a crude, rough-lumber building.

Some of the other business places which fell before the sweeping flames were a confectionery store owned by D. S. Thomas; a restaurant owned by John Cowgood; the Park Hotel, owned by N. E. Sargent; the F. E. Turrell Drug

Store; and a livery barn and equipment owned by E. C. Lake, known as Mayor Lake by the townspeople.

The E. Blackmore Meat Market was also destroyed as well as a number of freight and flat cars on the Manistee and Northeastern Railroad, plus the depot and nearly a half mile of track.

After the fire had burned itself out and the firemen had stopped its progress in the lumber piles and cooperage stock, and with most of the village in embers, a sudden panic struck. Food stocks and personal possessions were gone and the few remaining homes could not accommodate the homeless. Over a hundred buildings had burned.

Traverse City residents and merchants, however, rallied to the cause immediately and sent food and clothing. Subscriptions of money poured in from all directions and it was only a short while before the village began to rebuild.

But Lake Ann had seen its heyday. The new business places were scattered and some of them were poorly built. Then, in 1914, fire struck again and the business section was once more, in great part, destroyed. This fire, however, was not so serious because the village wasn't as closely knit and as large as in 1897. Four years passed and, for a third time, flames swept the business section. Again the Traverse City Fire Department was called but the damage was lasting. Lake Ann never recovered.

Today there are two stores, a restaurant, a town hall, a church and a scattering of homes, most of them resort buildings on the shore of the lake. The postoffice is in the larger of the two store buildings which was rebuilt on the foundation where Habbler first erected his general store.

Today, a group of Lake Ann residents, people who lived there when the village was young, are planning to write a history of the community. They have formed a historical society and are collecting pictures, facts and figures. Lake Ann is going to relive its big moments—but only on paper.

Pioneering in Leelanau

The following article by Thomas T. Bates appeared in the Traverse City *Morning Record* on December 10, 1899. Bates was co-publisher of the newspaper. It is undoubtedly one of the most authentic documents regarding the early settlement of Leelanau County.

"PREVIOUS to the year 1847, there was not a white man living in all Leelanau County. From Cat Head Point to the present boundary of Benzie County, it was an unbroken forest, inhabited almost entirely by wild beasts. There were few Indians there at that time.

"On the Manitou Islands there were a very few people. Two small piers had been built for the accommodation of steamers that stopped there for wood. The one on the northern island was owned by a man named Pickard, while a Mr. Barton owned the one on the south. Two fishermen without families also lived on the north island and the lighthouse was kept by a man named Clark.

"South of the present boundary of Leelanau County, at the mouth of the Betsy [Betsie] River, Joseph Oliver, a white settler, lived with his Indian wife and supported his family by trapping and fishing.

"These, with the small settlement at Old Mission and a bare handful of men at Traverse City, formed the only white population anywhere near the county of Leelanau, when John Lerue, the first settler, took up his residence at Sleeping Bear Bay, now Glen Arbor, in 1848. He had gone first to the Manitous in search of health, leaving his family at their home in Chicago. Here he had begun a traffic with the Indians who visited the islands, and this business he moved to Sleeping Bear Bay.

"Meanwhile, Rev. George N. Smith, of the Congregational Church, who was conducting mission work among the Indians of the Black River country, in Ottawa County, had been disturbed in some way by a settlement of Hollanders who located near him. Just what the trouble was, history fails to say, but Rev. Smith was not long in making-up his mind to remove to some point on Grand Traverse Bay. Accordingly, in 1848, he, with a company of Indians of his congregation, visited the area and made a choice of location somewhat north of the present site of Northport. They settled there in 1849.

"About the same time, James McLaughlin, Indian farmer for the Waukazoo band of Ottawas at Old Wing, Allegan County, was ordered to the region of Grand Traverse Bay. He left the mouth of the Kalamazoo River May 27, 1849, with his family of six, including himself, and the family of his brother-in-law, Wm. H. Case, which included three persons, in the schooner *H. Merrill*, which was owned by McLaughlin.

"Proceeding to the present site of Holland, they took on board Rev. Smith and his family, making a total of fifteen persons who were coming to the wilds of Leelanau County. After a tempestuous voyage the party rounded Cat Head Point, and entered the bay, June 11, 1849.

"At the point previously selected, Rev. Smith landed, with his family. A drenching rain was falling and the prospect was gloomy indeed. Smith was tempted to doubt the divine guidance on which he always depended, but he still clung to the hope that he was led of the Lord, and prepared to make the best of things.

"The rest of the company that had come with him didn't like the location, and continued on to the present site of Northport, and, with the exception of the few there and at the settlement at Old Mission, Smith knew of no whites in all the region. Just back of the spot he had chosen, the seemingly impenetrable swamp shut him off on the land side, and the bay in front effectually barred him from communication with the rest of the world, for a time at least.

"It was a prospect that was calculated to unnerve a stout heart, but there was no cowardice in the pioneer minister, and he began at once the work of making the wilderness habitable.

"Meanwhile Mr. McLaughlin and Mr. Case were building a home, 19 × 19 feet in size, on a spot within the present village of Northport. This house stood for many years and was afterwards used as a store by White and Burbeck after Northport had grown to be quite a settlement.

"Soon a Congregational Church was organized among the whites, and for a long period of years Rev. Smith acted as its pastor, continuing the work until his death from exposure in the line of duty, April 5, 1881.

"The settlement at Waukazooville was hardly established when the settlers remembered that the Fourth of July was approaching, and being patriotic, they did not wish to let the day pass without fitting observance. They had no cannon and no flag, but they decided that they could do without the former if some plan could be devised to supply the latter. A sailor on board the *H. Merrill* the vessel that had brought the party to the bay, came to the rescue. With a red flannel shirt and a white sheet, he made a flag that the settlement voted good enough for the celebration. All the guns of the party were made to do service as cannons, and all was ready when Independence Day dawned. The sunrise was greeted with a volley of guns, and the whole settlement went to the small island [Gull Island] in the bay, where a patriotic though not very elaborate celebration was held.

"That autumn preparations were made by the settlement for a long hard winter, but they were agreeably surprised by a very mild season. No snow fell until Dec. 12, and that was gone and the ground in good condition for cultivation by the first of April.

"The next season was a hard one. The crops, of course, were meager, as the settlers had had little time for clearing ground. The vessel that was to have brought their supplies was wrecked, and their supplies were very low. A long hard winter followed, and the settlers were near starvation when spring arrived.

"The next summer, John Dorsey came to join the family of Mr. Lerue at Glen Arbor. But in the fall of the same year, Mr. Lerue and Mr. McLaughlin removed to Elk Rapids, where he (Lerue) was building the saw mill for A. S. Wadsworth. In the spring of 1852, Mr. Lerue and family went back to their home at Glen Arbor, leaving but two families of white people at Northport; those of Mr. Smith and Mr. Case.

"In 1853, A. Mansoau located at the mouth of Carp River, on the present site of Leland. He was followed in 1854 by J. I. Miller, John Porter, H. S. Buckman, John Bryant, Sr., and Frederick Cook. Plans were at once set in motion for the construction of a pier and a sawmill, although they were not built for some time.

"In 1854, John E. Fisher of Fond-du-Lac, Wisconsin, came to Glen Arbor.

He was followed by his family, and that of his brother-in-law, a Mr. Cogswell, from New York state, and the next year by Dr. W. H. Walker, also of Fond-du-Lac, George Bay and a man by the name of Nutt, from Ohio. A pier was built on the spot afterward occupied by the dock owned by Charles Rossman.

"Soon after the departure of the families of Lerue and McLaughlin from Northport, other settlers began to arrive. Deacon Dame came from Old Mission and was the first to open business. He began the construction of a dock that was afterwards finished by H. O. Rose.

"It is of interest to note the condition of the settlers in the year 1885. The dock was still incomplete, the top being covered with poles instead of planks. There was no saw mill, as Mr. Voice had just begun the construction of the first one and it did not begin operating until the following year. There was no road leading from the village except the one to the little Indian settlement three miles up the shore. There was not a horse in the village, and but three yoke of oxen. Only one steamer touched at the half built pier, a small vessel plying between Grand Haven and Buffalo. The entire population of the settlement consisted of the families of the following: Joseph Dame, H. O. Rose, Amos Fox, William Voice, Capt. Peter Nelson, A. B. Page, S. W. Wilson, Thomas Retford, J. M. Burbeck, O. L. White, Henry Boyes, A. C. Stevens, Theodore Woodruff, Hiram Beckwith, Jesse Morgan, William Gill, and William Thomas.

"The first frame structure in the village was in the form of an addition, 14 × 20 feet in size, to a log house. The first entire frame house was built in 1856 by Mr. Thomas, for Mr. Woodruff.

"In 1856, the firm of White and Burbeck began the construction of a dock about three miles north of Northport, where they also engaged in the business of selling wood, tan bark and cedar posts.

"Mr. Rose was the first treasurer of the township of Leland, which at that time included all of the present counties of Leelanau and Benzie. He relates how he traveled all over the township, going as far south as the present village of Glen Arbor, to collect the tax, which was somewhat less than $600.

"Such was the beginning of the county of Leelanau . . . . There is little to suggest the old days in the thriving population that now fills the county. Pleasant villages, beautiful churches, modern schools, thriving farms and orchards, have removed the unbroken wilderness."

Bingham

THE VILLAGE of Bingham, today nothing more than a crossroads, was once a progressive and bustling community in Leelanau County. Located near the east shore of Lower Lake Leelanau (Carp Lake) it had, at the peak of its popularity, a population of about four hundred. There were a postoffice, stores, a blacksmith shop, a church, a saloon and a big sawmill.

Prior to 1880 there was a scattering of homes in the Bingham area but no village. The first sign of a settlement was in 1881 when Boone and Johnson bought a sawmill located near Nessen City and hired Louis Jessup and W. L. Fisher to move it to the shore of Carp Lake. Boone and Johnson had a financial interest in the mill, but the title was in the name of Samuel Charles Darrow.

The first log was cut into lumber on Christmas Eve, 1881, and Darrow began operations on a large scale. The first year's cut, however, was a disappointment. Darrow owed his mill crew and many other accounts, including stumpage costs. The money for the payment of these debts was to have come from the sale of the number-one hardwood lumber which was stacked in the yard. This had been loaded into a ship belonging to Hannah, Lay and Company, Traverse City, and taken to Chicago. After a wait of many days word came from Hannah, Lay and Company that the shipment was mildewed and unfit for use. In addition to this bad news, Darrow was billed for the shipping costs. When he settled his accounts he had a wagon, a horse and the clothes he and his family had on their backs.

But despite hectic years in the lumbering industry, the village of Bingham continued to grow. There was a postoffice in the store owned by Mike Oberlin and a saloon which was originally operated by Walter Moshier and later by Clint Richards. Two other stores handling general staples were operated by the Ancer and Gillem families. Three boarding houses provided for the lumberjacks and sawmill crewmen. A blacksmith shop was owned and operated by Zim (Zimri) Hinshaw.

Social life centered around the weekly dance in the hall near the center of the village. John Foote was a popular fiddler, and his sister, Clara Foote, played the organ. Then there was an Indian fiddler named John Manitou, who also provided dancing music and was a lot of fun for the young folks. Later, the combination of Foote and Johnson provided the music for the village frolics.

When Darrow lost out in the lumbering business there was danger that Bingham would die out. The Hannah-Lay interests, however, took over and operated the establishment and, in a short time, the mill was in normal production, prior to its sale to John Larkin. Later owners were the Barker Cedar Company, Mike Oberlin and Herb Boughy. It was dismantled by Boughy.

There is a story about how John Larkin bought the mill which is, without doubt, true. It was typical of the business methods used by Perry Hannah, of Hannah, Lay and Company. The story indicated that John Larkin was in business in some other area and was wiped out by a fire. He arrived in Traverse City broke and asked Perry Hannah if he could get credit to buy an axe so he could get a job in the woods. Hannah offered Larkin the mill at Bingham on a promise to pay. And pay he did.

While John Larkin had the mill at Bingham the village had its most rapid growth.

Across the lake there was a settlement of Polish people and a number of the families moved to the Bingham side of the lake to be near the lumbering operations. The settlers called them Polanders. These later became the backbone of the agricultural enterprise of the community.

Among those who arrived before 1880, were the Peltons, the Byers, the Wilsons, the Shugarts, the Hockstads and a score of others. Along with them came the Hurlbuts, the Heimforths, the Cores, the Boones, the McFarlands, the Trudes, the Donners and the Fishers. These are only a few of the pioneer settlers.

As the community grew, school matters, of course, got prompt attention. A log building was erected a short distance south of the intersection of Highway 22 and County Road 618. Teachers were paid as little as $15.00 a month and took their meals and lodging where they were invited. The first teacher was a young

94

lady named Blodgett. Two teachers who are well remembered in the Grand Traverse area were Jennie Anderson and John Tweddle. Miss Anderson was a sister to the pioneer undertaker in Traverse City, William Anderson. Tweddle turned to law following his teaching days and practiced his profession in Traverse City until shortly before his death.

There was never a lack of religious instruction in Bingham. At an early date, 1868, Sabbath School was started in a private home and continued through the years, eventually being enlarged to become a ministerial charge. The Evangelical Church was constructed just before the turn of the century and filled a community need.

With the closing of the sawmill there was a rapid exodus from the village. Since the lumberjacks and mill hands were no longer there, business declined rapidly. The stores closed, a boarding house remained for a while on scant patronage but eventually closed, and the buildings of the village were either torn down or fell before the ravages of time.

Today there is not a sign that would indicate that there was ever a bustling village at the Bingham corners. A single grocery store, the Richards Grocery, operated on County Road 618 just south of the old settlement, is the only indication of bustle. A few of the old villagers have scattered to the farms of the community but more of them have just moved away. There are still many of the old family names to be found on the mailboxes along the crossroads.

The Settlement Disappeared

THE ROLLING hills, the fertile soil and
a bubbling spring-fed creek across the area are the same, and the same sun warms
the earth as of a century ago, and the showers moisten the soil to produce crops
today as then. Now and then Ed Hohnke, or others who farm the location,
plow up an old stone axe, an arrowhead, or an ancient musket.

In this pretty section of north-central Leelanau County was once located the
Settlement. Different from most of the early settlements, this one was populated
entirely by Indians.

Why the Chippewas happened to stop in this area is not a matter of record.
It is only a short jaunt to Lake Leelanau in one direction and a short distance to
Lake Michigan in another. That might have been the reason the braves decided
to quit wandering and settle down.

At any rate, the story of the Settlement is one of the most interesting to be
uncovered in the Grand Traverse region. The main part of the Indian settlement
was located on property now owned by Ed Hohnke, earlier owned by his
parents.

Ottillia Hohnke first came to this country in 1878. She made the trip from
her native Poland with matrimony in mind. Arriving in America, she was wed
to August Hohnke and they made their home in Leelanau County.

It was a rugged spot in the wilderness with the only store across Carp Lake,
now Lake Leelanau, at the Bingham settlement. Later the Courturiers, owners
of the store, moved it to Provemont, now the village of Lake Leelanau.

That was the beginning of the story. The rest came from the sharp memory
of Mrs. Hohnke who lived to nearly the century mark, passing away in 1955.

The Hohnkes made friends with the Indians in the Settlement. Their farm was in the very center of the collection of Indian log cabins, bark huts and tattered lean-to shacks. Just west of the Hohnke farm home was a large log warehouse where the Chippewas stored a small amount of corn, dried and salt fish, salt venison and bows and arrows.

Three Ottawa chieftains from Leelanau County, around the turn of the century. Left to right, they are: Shawandase (Southern Clime), Wahsaqum (Clear Ice), and Abunggeshemok (Sundown).

Chief of the tribe was William Jake, the last Indian of the Settlement Grandma Hohnke remembered seeing. They were good people, those Indians, and kind, she recalled. They lived, actually, from day to day. They were happy if they could trade a basket of fish for a loaf of homemade bread, or sell a dozen beautiful baskets for 25 cents each.

To show their kindness they gave August Hohnke a great horn on which he could blow a loud blast to call for help. The kind of help Hohnke usually needed was aid in rounding up his strayed cattle. One blast from the horn, Mrs. Hohnke recalls, and there would be an Indian behind every bush and tree, peering out, wondering what the emergency was.

The Settlement had its "character" as most villages do. "Devil Jake" didn't have a first name unless one could find it in the state prison records at Jackson. He was a scalawag of the first water.

Mrs. Hohnke recalls an incident in which the "Devil" went through the woods to Northport cutting the tails off all the cattle he could catch en route. His string of meanness ran out, however, when he hit Charley "Somebody" in the head with an axe and was sent to prison for murder. While behind bars he got religion, and later when on parole, he returned to the Settlement. He spent his first night home with the August Hohnkes. When they arose in the morning he was gone. So was August's razor, his pistol, and the family silverware. A short time later "Devil Jake" was killed while felling a large hemlock tree near Glen Arbor.

The Settlement had its division-of-labor employment program. For instance, there were carpenters, as we would call them today. Their job was to make arrows, strip black ash for baskets and peel birch trees for bark canoes. Two of the men who boasted a carpenter's skill were John Wessma and Peter Peshanau.

Old Pete used to say, "Indian smarter than white man. Can peel birch bark and no crack it."

Indian children romped over the wooded hills and played their own games— maybe Indians and White Men. They gathered nightly in a large clearing near the Hohnke home to sing with the adults and romp with their playmates. Came time to sleep, they curled up wherever they happened to be, and likely enjoyed untroubled slumber.

Indians, cattle and wild animals drank from a common spring which still flows a full stream of water, giving head to a creek which crosses the Hohnke farm. It was the belief of the Indians that the spring held great curative powers and foot travelers from miles around came to carry away gallons of the water.

Sanitation in the Settlement was not good by any standard. This may, or may not, have led to its sudden end. Very young children often would be wrapped in skins, or old clothing, for two or three days at a time.

The Settlement was wiped out almost overnight. Without warning an epidemic of smallpox struck. The older Indians died first. They died so fast that the healthy members of the tribe could not bury them. Some of them crawled away into the woods to die alone. Whole families were wiped out within a few days. Many of the children were herded away to other settlements—Northport and Peshawbestown. A few of the more rugged individuals lived.

The neighboring white homesteaders set fire to the shacks, cabins and tents.

98

Every mark of the Settlement is gone except a single log cabin in the Hohnke yard, which, made from giant cedar logs, remains as a monument to the Indians who once roamed the area.

Today there are scores of souvenirs of the Settlement in the homes of the county. They have been turned up by plowshares, washed up by rain, or found on top of the earth by playing children.

Burdickville—Alone on Glen Lake

ONLY ONE village recognized as such and boasting a postoffice ever existed on the shore of Glen Lake. It was Burdickville, puny child of the timber days, which hardly got out of the swaddling clothes of infancy before it became a memory.

Leelanau County, being a peninsula, was not favorably located for extensive development in the early days. Despite the fact that there were countless thousands of feet of timber on her rolling hills, no extensive settlement was made until several years after the first white settlers came to the Grand Traverse area.

In 1851, John Dorsey arrived at the site of Glen Arbor, paving the way for a village at that point. Ten years prior to that date, there was a settlement, although very small, at the present site of Northport. At other points over the county, there was, here and there, a family of pioneers, either farming or conducting minor trade operations with the Indians and scattered white hunters and trappers.

It was about 1857 that William Burdick decided to build a small sawmill on the shore of Glen Lake. The site he selected was in a section densely covered with both hardwood and pine. In connection with his lumber manufacturing operation, he erected a grist mill to serve the residents of the county, for the nearest grist mill was in Traverse City. He operated the sawmill for about ten years before it burned to the ground (1869). However, it was established long enough to give the nucleus of a settlement a name: Burdickville.

For a time, after the Burdick mills burned, it seemed highly probable that the village would disappear. Two years prior to the fire, a man named John Helm had established a general store and it was around this store that the remainder of the life of the town was centered. Helm, who had a varied career prior to his settling in Leelanau County, was ambitious and intelligent. He had served with the Sixteenth Illinois Infantry during the Civil War and later, as a civilian, served under General Stanley as a quartermaster. In 1865, he took up a homestead and also, in the fall of 1865, opened a small store in the village of Glen Haven.

Feeling that there was a bright future for a village at the site of Burdickville, in 1867 he moved his store to that place. His stock of goods was small but met the needs of the scattered population. Staples were flour, salt meat (mess pork), beans, salt, molasses and kerosene. Of course, there were other items in the grocery line but they were not in great demand. Also, there was clothing that was needed.

An interesting sidelight in the history of the town concerns a gentleman by the name of Silas Doty, better known as Sile Doty. Sile was locally acclaimed the greatest and most successful sneak-thief, robber and cutthroat of the century. Unlike most of his kind, he died a respected man after serving some time in prison for both robbery and murder. How Sile became involved in local history is easy to understand. He had a sister living in Burdickville and, when the going got a little too hot in southern Michigan, where he carried on a majority of his operations, he would head north until the uproar quieted down.

The Helm store, at times, was left unattended. Everyone was trustworthy in the community and, if Helm happened to step out for a few minutes, there was little cause to worry. It so happened that Sile Doty once had finished spending a few days in the home of his sister and was ready to move on. On his way out of town he stopped in at the Helm store while Helm was in another part of the building. Helm returned just in time to see Sile disappear with two satchels stuffed with bulky matter.

The Helm store was, for its time, a pretentious building near the shore of Glen Lake. On the second floor, there was room for a dance hall where many of the community events were held. Unlike most villages of that day, there was neither church nor saloon in the village. Nannie A. Helm, Helm's daughter, recalls that there was plenty of liquor available from outside sources, but none, to her knowledge, was ever sold in the village.

In 1868, a postoffice was established and the mail arrived by pack about two times a week after the service was established. Helm was named postmaster.

Nan Helm recalls that mail was usually carried by an Indian runner. In 1876, Helm resigned as postmaster, and his wife, Nancy, was appointed. She was, as far as can be determined, the first woman postmaster in the state of Michigan. Despite political changes, she remained postmistress for about 35 years.

The Helm family operated their general store for nearly half a century. The original little log store and the two-floor building are gone. The original store was used as a storage building for a number of years; the big one burned to the ground shortly after Helm sold it.

In 1871, S. S. Burnette brought a stock of merchandise to the village and opened a competitive business. The Burnette store was a slab structure and at no time was a serious threat to the Helm prosperity. It was located directly across from the Helm building. It, too, is long gone. Mrs. Burnette was an ardent gardener and planted roses all over her tiny tract of land. Those rose plants have spread and are still blooming each spring, a monument to a pioneer woman and her love for beauty.

Among the old records of the county, one can find the plat of Burdickville. On it one can find a Prospect Avenue and an Agnew Drive. The pioneers have all moved on. There isn't as much as a foundation to mark the site of the village. The chapel, built long after the village was established, still stands and has been turned into a museum for Leelanau County. A beautiful public park has been established near the spot where the old Helm store once stood—a fitting monument to the people who fought the wilderness.

Glen Arbor: A Link with the Past

AT THE base of a gentle bay which sags the shoreline of Leelanau County south of the Manitou Islands, and between Sleeping Bear Point on the west and Pyramid Point on the east, lies the little village of Glen Arbor. It is a quiet and progressive place with a majority of the population being summer residents.

However, there was a time when Glen Arbor was as up-and-coming a town as you would wish to find. For instance, there was the Todd Hotel and Livery and the F. A. Earl Jewelry Store; there were grocery and drygoods stores, a smithy and several mills. There was even a railroad which started at the head of Little Glen Lake and wound around through sections 20, 30, 19 and 21. The railroad was a narrow-gauge, and the engine, which hauled edging, lumber and wood, was imported for that purpose by the Nessen mill. The engine was later sold to the D. H. Day Lumber Company and now stands in Clinch Park in Traverse City.

The history of Glen Arbor, to a great extent, lies buried in an old and abandoned graveyard near the village. Here, in unmarked graves, lie scores of men and women who helped settle the village and carve it out of the pine and hardwood.

The first settlers to arrive at the site of the village were John E. Fisher, John Dorsey and John LaRue. Known among the later arrivals as the "three Johns," these men were the pioneer inspiration which later brought a great number of settlers. They arrived about 1854. John Helm may have been one of the early "Johns."

The first steamer to put in at Glen Arbor was the *Saginaw*. George Ray, who had pre-empted a considerable amount of land in the area, returned to his home in Ohio, bought a sawmill, loaded it on the *Saginaw*, along with household goods, two cows and a lot of miscellaneous items; and headed back to Glen Arbor. That was in 1855. Later Glen Arbor was to develop into a wooding place for the propellor ships which began to ply the Great Lakes with increasing frequency.

Glen Arbor, when it was first started, was not located where it now stands. It was further northward and directly on the shore of the Lake Michigan. After one winter on the wind-swept shore, the pioneers, hardy though they were, began to wish they had built a little farther inland and behind a windbreak of giant pine trees. It was only a matter of time before this move was made, albeit gradually.

Today, only one of the pioneer buildings of the original Glen Arbor still stands. It is a vacant and weatherbeaten shell which was variously used as a grocery store, town hall, drygoods store, storage house and jewelry store operated for some time by F. A. Earl.

As for the second and present site, only one residential building still stands, unaltered, as it was built in the pioneer day. It is the home of Mrs. Etta May Todd, eighty-four, who was born and raised in the sprawling old building.

The actual naming of Glen Arbor has caused considerable speculation among would-be historians. It has been variously conceded that the name is a corruption of Glen Harbor. Such is not the case.

The village was named by Mrs. John E. Fisher, grandmother of Mrs. Todd. It came about that when the early settlers arrived, the heavily wooded area was in its peak of foliage. The spot where it was decided to start building was a shaded glen with towering pines and hardwoods on all sides. Entwined in the tops of the trees was an almost impenetrable mass of wild grape vines. That was it. Mrs. Fisher said it was a glen arbor created by nature. And Glen Arbor it still is.

George Ray, who brought the first steamer into the harbor, was also the first school teacher and the first official postmaster. The postoffice was established shortly after his arrival. While Mr. Ray was the first postmaster appointed by the federal government there was a sort of postoffice in operation before that. A giant hollow tree stood near the center of the present village and near an old Indian council ground. It was the custom for persons wishing to post letters, to place them in this hollow tree, and the runner, when the spirit moved him, would collect them and take them to the nearest postoffice, usually to Traverse City.

While it is impossible, in a limited space, to discuss more than a few of the pioneer residents of the Glen Arbor community, one man, who helped greatly in the early struggle of the village, must not be omitted. He is Dr. William H. Walker. There is considerable doubt about the statement that he arrived at the harbor with John Fisher, but there is no doubt about the influence he exerted on the community. Soon after his arrival he noticed the possibility of producing cranberries on a tract of bog land which was located on the edge of the village. For the good doctor to think was to act, and he established berries in the marsh to such an extent that it was a thriving industry for many years. He built barracks to house his pickers and erected a beautiful home on a knoll overlooking his buildings. The house, like Dr. Walker, is gone. He was buried on a high point of land by his cranberry marsh and a large marker stands over his grave.

First church services in Glen Arbor were held in the home of Schoolmaster Ray in 1856. The worship was conducted by Rev. Charles E. Bailey. The first political meeting was also held in the Ray home and was called by J. C. Ramsdell and R. J. Ramsdell, who later became important political figures in western Michigan.

From 1855 to 1875 there was a tremendous logging business. Tom Kelderhouse built a dock, and such names as McCarty, Dumbrille, Pickard, Miller, Nessen and many others made lumbering history in the region. D. H. Day, who had his vast holdings, was one of the first of the pioneers to appreciate the value of selective timber harvest. The result of his forethought can still be seen in the Day Forest Estate.

At the edge of the village of Glen Arbor is an abandoned and overgrown cemetery. Only a few graves can be identified. Trees have grown about them and a tangle of underbrush makes walking difficult. A patch of myrtle, once a decoration for someone's grave, has spread across the cemetery roadway. Here and there a rusted G.A.R. sign can be seen. Memory of many of the people who lie there is gone. The cemetery tells a part of the history of the village, which should be salvaged and, in some way, somehow, made to live again in the minds of the present residents.

Glen Arbor, today, has a postoffice, stores, gasoline stations and gift shops.

Where scores of black bears once roamed (Glen Lake was once called Bear Lake) there are picnic tables, summer cottages and roads which wind through the still wooded area.

At a point where "Old Man" Foster platted a piece of property at the mouth of the Crystal River there is a private secondary school of national acclaim. It is the Leelanau Schools.

Glen Lake, even as far back as 1885, has been said to be as beautiful as Italy's Lake Como.

The landscape hasn't changed in the past century. But there are no lumberjacks in the eating places, and the fiddle and the harmonica no longer give out with "Turkey in the Straw" at the ramshackle town hall. Glen Arbor is just another village with a past.

The Leelanau Schools

ON THE shore of Lake Michigan at the mouth of Crystal River, in Leelanau County, is located another local institution of learning which has gained recognition across the country.

The Leelanau Schools had a modest beginning. William and Cora Beals arrived in picturesque Leelanau County in 1923 to establish a summer camp for boys. On their property at the mouth of the river, there were but two buildings, a cottage and a small shack used by commercial fishermen for cleaning their catches. Yet, with the addition of a couple of canvas covered cabins, a camp was founded.

In 1929 in addition to Camp Leelanau for Boys the school was created and was known as Leelanau for Boys. The Skipper, as William Beals was affectionately known to the students, had a way of doing things which seemed impossible. That is the reason why a modern school has developed from a humble summer camp.

Parents learned the value of the progressive educational system incorporated into the private school. Too, many of them wanted their daughters to benefit from the training which Skipper Beals and Cora had created. Thus, in 1940 Pinebrook for Girls was also established, and since the schools were co-educational, they were known as The Leelanau Schools.

From its first forty acres of land, it has spread to a total of 750 acres. Independent in its teaching approach, the school is accredited by the University of Michigan.

In addition to the standard subjects, the school offers courses in many of the arts—in music and in painting.

The untimely death of The Skipper in 1942 brought about a change in leadership. Arthur Huey, one of the top faculty members, accepted the reins and, assisted by Mrs. Beals who remains as business manager, the school continues to forge ahead.

It is another example of the cultural pioneering that is found so often in sections of our country where men have carved a civilization out of a wilderness.

Shady Trails

ON A STRIP of land in Leelanau
County, on the west shore of the west arm of Grand Traverse Bay, purchased
directly from the Ahgosa family, is located another monument to cultural
advancement in the Grand Traverse region. It is Shady Trails, a school devoted
to speech correction and improvement. Before the coming of the school, the
spot was known as Ahgosatown and is still described as such on some old maps.

The institution was founded by Mr. and Mrs. John N. Clancy in 1932, when
Clancy, himself a recovered stutterer, assisted by his wife, Grace, decided that
youngsters with speech problems could be cured, and thus was born Shady
Trails. With only four students in 1932, the institution has since grown to become the outstanding one of its type in the nation. In the spring of 1949, through
a gift from the Kresge Foundation, it became a part of the University of
Michigan.

It was the pioneer spirit of John Clancy, a native of the Grand Traverse
region, that brought into being, and kept alive during the "rough years," a
priceless cultural institution.

Eagletown

THE FIRST real records of Eagletown are found in a church book begun in 1852 when a mission there was opened by Father Angelus VanPaemel. In the baptismal register of the Immaculate Conception Mission Church (Peshawbestown, Leelanau County), lies a story that can only be appreciated by a careful scanning of its tattered pages.

It was a scrawny mission which had, as its nucleus, a group of Ottawa Indians who had moved into the region from Harbor Springs in 1845.

In 1855, Father Ignatius Mrack took over the mission and, in his first writings, he refers to the settlement as Eagletown. His mission covered a wide territory and ranged beyond the bounds of the Grand Traverse region. Baptismal records, death records, a chronology of local events, all are inscribed in the church book in the cramped handwriting of Father Mrack. Much of the writing is in Latin.

In 1883, Rev. Philip Zorn, who had succeeded Father Mrack as pastor of the mission, referred to the settlement as Peshaube, after a taciturn old Ottawa chieftain who ruled the Indians of the settlement. The original name of Eagletown is not mentioned in the church book of that date, and the place was referred to as Peshawbestown from 1895 on when Father Brune Torka arrived to minister to the spiritual needs of the Indians of the mission.

Father Torka was the first of a long line of Franciscans who worked with the Indians in the Lower Peninsula. Headquarters for the Franciscans was in Petoskey. For more than a half century the Peshawbestown mission was operated by the Petoskey group. Mission priests from the Petoskey headquarters were Fathers Brune Torka, Innocent Schleuter, Siegfried Rinderman, Donulus Evers, Albert Bruesserman, Dorotheus Philipp, Arnold Schwarz, Aubert Keuter, Emmerman Fox, Connall Berube and Clemantine Croskoff.

In 1948, the Peshawbestown mission was removed from the jurisdiction of the Petoskey Franciscans and attached to the Suttons Bay parish under the pastorate of Father Charles Baker. Later in the same year, it was assigned to the Gills Pier parish under the pastorate of Father William Hoogterp.

In 1950, there began a modern renaissance of the mission when Father Joseph Sakowski took charge. Interest in the church and the community has grown in the ensuing years.

The church, destroyed once by fire and rebuilt in 1886, is not an imposing structure. The original building was blessed by Father Ignatius Mrack. In 1886, he returned to work at the mission after being elevated to carry the bishop's seal and, that same year, blessed the new building, which still is in use.

The windows in the service section of the building are collectors' items. In that early day the builders were interested in getting light into the structure and cared little about the view through the panes of glass. For that reason they were satisfied with "poured" panes rather than with the more costly drawn or rolled glass. The wavy structure of the glass makes it impossible to see through many of the windows.

One item in the Peshawbestown church that is somewhat of a mystery is a collection of paintings in a back room. There is no written record of how the half dozen pictures came to be there but tradition has it that they were brought to this country from Czechoslovakia by Bishop Frederick Baraga. One of the works is of exceptional quality and in good condition and should be framed and restored to a place of honor in the church.

A new era of mission work is being carried on in the Peshawbestown Indian reservation. A troop of Boy Scouts has been organized. The church recreation quarters is used almost nightly by various groups. Sewing clubs, 4-H clubs, domestic science classes and other activities are well attended.

In front of the church, at the north end of the reservation, stands a large boulder bearing a plaque in bronze, setting forth the dates of the first mission. Someone took too much for granted, however, according to the Indians. The sponsors of the marker spelled the name of the reservation "Peshabatown" instead of Peshawbestown, as it should be.

The Omena Church

OGEMAHGIGEDO, a woman named Mary, Peneswageshik and Pashen were baptized on June 20, 1852. They were the first to be baptized and take communion at New Mission in Leelanau County, now called Omena.

The story of Omena, in its early days, is the story of the Presbyterian Church and its mission work. The New Mission Church, standing trim and white today, is a monument to the success of that pioneer effort.

Only once in the past seventy-five years have the lights been out on Christmas Eve. Since Rev. Peter Dougherty founded the mission in 1852 and supervised the construction of the church in 1858, there has been continuous Sunday school and Bible teaching.

The little church is not only a landmark, it is a page from history. Over its threshold have passed such Ottawa and Chippewa names as Ahgosa, Mamagoena, Ogemahgigedo, Waukazoo, Majewada, Panateen, Petoskey and Sahgahsega. It was here they heard the Rev. Dougherty read from the pages of the Bible and heard the words translated into their native tongues. Many of the Indians never learned to master the sounds of the English language.

The beginnings of the New Mission Church date back to the mid-1800's. At that time the Indians, Chippewas and a few Ottawas, were settled on Old Mission peninsula. It was here that Rev. Dougherty first established his work. Then the land was opened to settlement, and the Indians were forced to move. On advice from Rev. Dougherty, most of them moved to the point northwest across the west arm of Grand Traverse Bay. The migration took place in 1852, and it was in that year the first records show a mission established.

The church, as it now stands, was not built until about 1858, and, for the years between the founding of the New Mission and the erection of the place of worship, services were held in the manse, as the residence of the pastor was called. It served as a school for the Ottawa and Chippewa children and was a social center for many years.

The New Mission Church was built from lumber produced in a muley mill on the Milwaukee side of Lake Michigan and brought to the point by boat. It was originally built with two doors and no windows on the south elevation. At a later and undetermined date this was changed and a single door was placed in the center and windows were placed in the end of the building. Inside the church are the staid pews of another era. There is about the church a quiet dignity and a restful atmosphere.

The door of the building is never locked. It is open, ever, as though beckoning a weary pioneer or a copper-skinned brave, tired from a hunting trip.

The great bell, hidden from view in the steeple on the church, is an item of much sentiment. It was cast from a large copper penny collection from the Indians and is a tribute to the leadership of the doughty Rev. Dougherty.

Rev. Dougherty, and one can almost see him at the altar of the little church, was a small man. He was pudgy and serious of mind. Sharp blue eyes and a mop of dark hair added to his look of leadership.

The Indians of the settlement had a name for him. They called him Mickoos, or Mikoos, whichever spelling one wished. It meant Little Beaver.

Another name which tradition, and near-legend, says was given the good reverend was "Omena." In the language of the Indians, it meant "Is it so?" Historians tell us that this was a favorite expression used by Dougherty when speaking with an Indian. That, too, is believed to be the true origin of the name of the village of Omena. Grand Traverse County was once, before 1851, called Omena County.

Rev. Dougherty came to Old Mission on the peninsula of Grand Traverse County to teach the Chippewa Indians. He found himself teaching a mixture of Chippewas and Ottawas. Chief Ahgosa and Chief Aishquaqwanaba were Chippewas and powerful Indian leaders. It would seem that a major portion of the disciples of his Presbyterian mission were of that tribe.

There is mention twice in available records of a tribe of Peshawba Indians living on the Old Mission peninsula. It is also recorded that they were a tribe of the Chippewa nation. However, after the migration of the Old Mission Indians to New Mission nothing more is mentioned of the group.

But, back to the New Mission at Omena. Each Sunday since the old building first took shape nearly a century ago, there has been a gathering of devout folks from the community. There have always been Sunday school and Bible classes in the structure.

Every year at Christmas time the building is decorated and a beautiful evergreen tree is set up on the platform. The youngsters, Indian and white, even as it was in the days of Rev. Dougherty, take part in the yuletide services.

The old manse has long been lost to the church. It was sold and became a summer hotel, the Omena Inn. A new manse was built just south of the church.

Claude Craker is caretaker of the church property, even as his father, George Craker and his grandfather were caretakers. The missionary work in the New Mission was as interwoven with the good works of the Craker family as with the Doughertys. They found their accomplishments good and they have lived on in the community.

W. A. Craker, many years active as superintendent of the Mission Sunday school, is nearing his ninety-first birthday. He is still active and interested in the community and each year is named superintendent emeritus of the Sabbath school. Ruth Craker, another descendant of the original stock, has written a very accurate history of the area.

George Craker came to Old Mission with Rev. Dougherty and, when the mission was moved, moved with it. He taught the Indians how to till the soil, build homes, and how to use tools. His good wife taught school at the New Mission. She showed the Indian girls how to cook, sew and become Christian housekeepers.

Many of the folks who worked at New Mission are still there. They lie buried in the tiny cemetery just east of the church. That is the way they would have wanted it. Indians of the Ottawa and Chippewa tribes worked and worshipped side by side. Now, as they wander in peace over their happy hunting grounds, their bodies rest side by side in death.

Louisville: A Pagan Village

I WALKED today with Jonas Shawandasa over the site of the old pagan Indian village of Louisville and stood beside an Indian burial ground, near Northport, in Leelanau County, which Jonas said was probably three hundred years old.

Jonas Shawandasa can trace his family back at least two hundred years and the history of his family is the history of the Leelanau County area. He was born near Northport, as were his father and mother before him, and his life, like theirs, has been local Indian history.

The story of Louisville is intriguing. There is nothing in history books about it and nothing in historical records.

The Louisville settlement once stood on a high bluff overlooking Lake Michigan at a point where Petersen Park is now located, about two miles north of the village of Northport. In the beginning it was composed of scores of bark shacks which housed a band of "unbelievers" of the Ottawa tribe. While an overwhelming majority of the natives believed in the Great Spirit, the Ottawas at Louisville did not.

There is no record of the beginning, or the end, of the settlement. Earlier, it had an Indian name which had been lost, Jonas recalled. About a century ago it took the name of Louisville after a resident, Louis Kookosh, whose name, literally translated, means Louis the Pig.

Not one regional person in a round thousand knows where the village stood and even fewer know where the village burial ground, unhallowed and unmarked, is located.

The cemetery, if such it can be called, can be reached by parking at the entrance of Petersen Park and walking to the right about a quarter of a mile, skirting an area of second growth, and then a few rods to the right. There are no markers over the graves and nothing to indicate that scores of bodies lie beneath the sod. Sunken spots indicate individual graves. A tangle of rusted barbed wire lies in the grass, which once, many years ago, kept livestock from grazing the spot. Some of the burial ground has been plowed up and its area reduced until, today, there is only a spot about fifty by forty-five feet remaining.

Here are buried the remains of Indians who lived untrammeled lives before the American Revolution. They lived from the land and returned to the land. Even Jonas Shawandasa has no idea as to how many graves were originally in the area or whose they might have been. It was abandoned before his time as was the village of Louisville. Part of the village was located on a farm belonging to Archie Scott, where the cemetery is situated.

It is certain that the cemetery antedated the one at Onominee, about five miles from the village of Northport. It is in this latter one that Jonas' parents, Louis and Sarah Shawandasa, are buried. Here too, are the remains of scouts of the Indian wars, veterans of the Sioux uprising, two Civil War veterans and scores of others. Not many of the graves are marked and there are only memories, fast being taken away, to keep the page of the book readable.

The name Shawandasa means southward and refers to anything south, such as a trip, a home or a place.

Jonas speaks the Ottawa language fluently.

"The young folks don't speak it," he explained, "and the older ones are leaving. I almost forgot the language for many years and then I began using it."

It is a pretty language: soft like French, musical like Spanish and with a force not unlike Yankee English. It is spoken today by a few and read by fewer.

If you would like to spend an hour of enchantment, or step back into history, visit Jonas and walk with him over the soil where once stood the pagan village of Louisville. Hear him speak of his ancestors, among them chieftains, and look with him as he stands on the bluff and points toward the Manitous.

MONUMENT
TO THE
SPIRIT

Intrigue, political maneuvering, under-the-table tactics, and physical combat played an important part in one of the most bitterly fought county-seat struggles ever brought to light in the history of the state of Michigan. It was for the location of the county government of Wexford County.

Sherman, Intrigue in the Wilderness

INTRIGUE, political maneuvering, under-the-table tactics, and physical combat played an important part in one of the most bitterly fought county-seat struggles ever brought to light in the history of the state of Michigan. It was for the location of the county government of Wexford County.

Sherman, an isolated village twenty-six miles south of Traverse City on M-37, and north of Mesick, had its beginnings in the year of 1867 when Lewis J. Clark opened a store on the banks of the Manistee River, near the present site of the M-37 bridge. In 1868, he moved to the corners where the village of Sherman was to be built.

That same year, a postoffice was established with John Perry as postmaster. In 1869, Clark was appointed postmaster and the office was moved to his general store. There was a succession of postmasters: E. W. Stewart, J. S. Walling, C. E. Cooper, H. B. Sturtevant, H. F. Campbell, and J. H. Wheeler.

Also, in 1869, Sylvester Clark kept a hotel in his log home, and the Maqueston brothers, Edward and Isaac, opened a general store. In connection with his hotel, Clark operated a stage coach line and Mrs. Clark served meals in the establishment. During 1872, he expanded his business interests and opened a drug store.

H. B. Sturtevant was the first school teacher in the rude building which opened during the winter of 1869 and 1870. The next winter he taught classes in a building occupied jointly by the school and the prosecuting attorney.

T. A. Ferguson was the first attorney to hang his shingle in Sherman. He opened his office in 1869.

In 1869, Sherman was named county seat of Wexford County and in 1872, a courthouse was constructed. The next summer a jail was built. The courthouse stood on the west side of M-37 where the Sherman village park is now located, and the jail was a short distance north of the courthouse.

By 1872, Sherman village had grown to a point where there was need of a newspaper. The *Wexford County Pioneer* was established and the first copies came off the press in the spring of that year. The paper was owned by Cooper and

Courthouse, Sherman. Around this staid building swirled one of the most violent county seat battles in Michigan. It was once the county capital of Wexford County, but eventually Manton got to be the county seat, and then Cadillac.

Tucker and went through a succession of ownerships as follows: Charles Cooper, Charles Marr, Campbell and Wheeler, and J. H. Wheeler. Wheeler owned the paper when, as the *Sherman Pioneer*, the last issue was printed on May 3, 1912.

In 1872, the village was composed of twenty families plus the business places. The following year, with mushroom growth, the village had between two hundred and fifty and three hundred residents.

One of the big needs of the village was a gristmill. A group of residents pooled their resources to the extent of $1,000 to be used toward the acquisition of such an enterprise. Several parties showed interest but, in 1877, a team named Shackleton and Bennett, Clam Lake (now Cadillac), stated that if an additional $200 could be secured, they would build. The money was raised and a mill was erected on the little creek just north of the village. The old dam still stands and the pond still holds a fine head of water. Production of good quality flour came from twin stones and a place was open for a third if the demand was sufficient. It was never installed.

Churches, societies, clubs and fraternal organizations were a part of the community.

The story of Sherman, however, is not in its rapid growth and its place as a community center and county seat of Wexford County. It is the story of its struggle for existence and to remain the county seat.

The first battle flag was waved in 1872 during the annual meeting of the county Board of Supervisors. It was during that meeting that Supervisor Hollister introduced a resolution to remove the county seat from Sherman to Clam Lake, a bustling village in the southeast corner of the county. The resolution was defeated by a vote of five to four. Thus was the die cast for a battle of "no-holds-barred" which was destined to last a decade.

In 1873, Hollister again renewed his efforts and his resolution was defeated by a vote of six to three.

The first evidence of political intrigue was displayed in 1873 when the township of Cleon, formerly a part of Manistee County, was attached to Wexford. This move was accomplished by virtue of a petition, circulated in Manistee, requesting the change. The messenger assigned to the petition related his methods later and stated that he would go into a bar, order a round of drinks for everyone and whip out the printed petition. Most of his obligated guests signed without reading. The first annexation was declared unconstitutional and it wasn't until late in 1873 that the state legislature finally approved the move. It remained a part of Wexford County until 1881 when it was returned to Manistee.

On June 14, 1876, two resolutions were presented to the Board of Supervisors for the removal of the county seat. Supervisor William Kelley proposed, again, the change to Clam Lake, and Warren Sherman, supervisor from Cedar

Creek Township, asked that it be established at Manton. Both resolutions lost in a tie vote: eight to eight.

In March, 1877, a telling blow was struck by Clam Lake. The village grew up and took on the status of a city. The name was changed to Cadillac and Cadillac gained three more votes on the Board of Supervisors.

Action was taken immediately by residents in the northern part of the county. They began the official formation of four new townships to counteract the additional power of the Clam Lake group. The new townships, with area taken from already established political boundaries, were to be known as West-side, Wheatland, Dover and Sherman. To speed the formation of these new townships before the three new votes in Cadillac proved disastrous, a special meeting of the Board of Supervisors was called for March 30, 1877, for official approval of the new districts. Fearing the board members from the southern part of the county would invoke stalling tactics, a rule was adopted that no member would be allowed to speak on the matter more than once. Thus, under a type of "gag rule," the new townships were organized.

The session was a hectic one. The board recessed at 7 p.m. and a special meeting was held by the board members from the northeast section of the county. The result was held secret until the board re-assembled for their evening session. This meeting was a hassel over the proposal to move the county seat to Manton. The Sherman supervisors would not yield and the Manton members threatened to reconsider the resolution which created four new townships.

Manton made good the threat and, when the meeting re-opened, called the resolutions, one by one, back to the table. When a proposal to move the county seat to Manton was brought up, the supervisors saw that they had been playing with fire by alienating the Sherman vote. An effort was then made to take the resolutions from the table but an immediate motion was made to adjourn.

S. S. Fallass, Clam Lake, later a Circuit Judge, took the floor during the squabble and began a discourse on his reason for voting as he did. His speech was a pioneer version of a filibuster. He droned on and on, read extracts from the state constitution and from state statutes. He declared that he would see Sunday's sunrise before he would admit the new townships. At 10 p.m. he sent out for supper which he ate between bursts of oratory.

He said he would yield the floor for no motion except a motion for immediate adjournment. He won his point and the meeting was adjourned. The new township proposal went by the board with the exception of the town of Sherman, which was approved.

Even with the new township of Sherman approved by the board, there was difficulty in getting a supervisor seated because of an arbitrary attitude on the part of the county clerk who would refuse to call his name. The clerk claimed that the township was illegal. Sherman residents took the matter to Circuit Court and won a seat on the board.

A new twist to the county seat battle was introduced in 1877 when a resolution was presented that would move the county seat to Dayhuff Lake, the geographical center of the county. Dayhuff Lake (now Meauataka) was an unsettled area and the lake at that time was drying up. This resolution died on the table. S. S. Fallass introduced a similar resolution the next month and it was defeated by a tie vote of nine and nine.

In June 1877, the supervisor from Cedar Creek Township introduced a resolution to move the county seat to Manton. Again a tie vote, nine to nine, killed the proposal.

In 1878, the village of Sherman saw the tide of battle go against them. A proposal to move the county seat to Manton received the needed two-thirds vote of the board of supervisors—thirteen to six. However, when it came up for ratification by vote of the people of the county, in April 1879, it was defeated by a vote of 971 against, and 290 for the change.

Then Cadillac residents, under the leadership of Col. T. J. Thorp, rallied around a decision that getting the county seat away from Sherman would be a first step in getting it to Cadillac. In essence, Col. Thorp said to the Manton people, "You introduce another resolution to move the county seat to your village to test the good faith of the people of Sherman and we will be as loyal to you as they have been."

Accordingly, on October 13, 1881, the seventeenth resolution was introduced regarding the location of the county government.

When the roll was called, sixteen supervisors voted for the change and two against. The residents of the north portion of the county had reached a conclusion that they might better fall in with the move to Manton or they would see the courthouse, eventually, moved to Cadillac. Cadillac residents felt that, once they had the capital on the move, it would be only a matter of time when they could win their battle of having it changed to the Clam Lake site.

Between the time of the action of the board of supervisors and the ratification by the people, Wexford County was a hotbed of barter for votes. Old-timers relate that physical combat was common in every section of the county and enmities developed between families, friends, and fellow workers.

When the matter finally came to a vote of the people, it was carried overwhelmingly in favor of Manton. The count was 1,255 for, and 146 against. Sherman had lost the county seat.

The story of the removal of the county records from Sherman to Manton was not a tale of love and marriage. The residents of the Sherman region were unhappy and, while there are no written records of the conflict, stories are still told of "knock-down-drag-out" fights in saloons and in the woods.

But Manton couldn't be smug in her victory. She was destined to be the county seat for only a short time.

Even before the county records were well settled in Manton, a new resolution was introduced before the Board of Supervisors. It was the eighteenth such resolution having to do with the county seat. This resolution was referred to the Committee on Towns and Counties and never reported out.

Now Cadillac residents went to work in earnest. Taking a leaf from the history of the Sherman scrapbook, they proposed to split up townships to give them an advantage of more votes on the board. Six new townships were proposed. Henry May, Cadillac, was elected to the legislature and he was successful in getting Cleon Township returned to Manistee County. It had served its purpose and its removal from Wexford would lessen the northern strength.

May also was successful in getting the township of Sherman "disorganized." This move gave Cadillac two less votes to oppose any move they might now make in moving the county seat. Sherman retaliated by efforts to organize two new townships, but the courts ruled the townships illegal.

The six new townships planned for the Cadillac area were Copley, Kysor, Garfield, Lindon, Long Lake and Nelson. While the matter of the formation of the new townships was still in committee, Supervisor J. R. Bishop, Cadillac, offered the nineteenth resolution on the county seat location. It was put to a vote of the board members and the balance of power was expected to defeat the resolution. When the ballots were counted, it was found that there was exactly a two-thirds majority in favor of moving the county capital to Cadillac. The deciding vote had been that of the supervisor from Liberty Township, adjoining the village of Manton, who had voted for the removal. No one ever knew why.

The newly proposed townships in Wexford were now declared, by the committee, to be "fatally defective" in their organization and to have no legal existence. They were no longer needed.

At the April election, 1882, the people of Wexford County approved the change by a vote of 1,363 to 636 and at break of day, on the morning following the election, a train arrived in Manton to remove the records.

The volunteers who accompanied the special train, though, were not prepared for the resistance they were to meet. The Cadillac men said the reason for the unseeming haste was to avoid the expense and delay of injunction proceedings which Manton had threatened. Manton rallied sufficient forces to turn back the "invaders." Undaunted, the train crew and volunteers returned to Cadillac, recruited campmen and mill hands to a force of about one hundred and fifty combat-minded individuals. Fortified with a few bottles of "beverage" they returned to Manton and succeeded in removing the county records. Oldsters recount it was a pitched battle.

In 1903, John Wheeler, publisher of the *Sherman Pioneer*, compiled a history of Sherman and her fight to retain the county seat. In his work, he recounted a few of the items of intrigue and corruption which took place during the decade of struggle.

"At times it [the fight] had been very bitter, and its inner history would reveal a vast deal more of corruption than it is worthwhile here to portray," he wrote.

Wheeler wrote of a few of the instances where evil practices were used. One was the occasion when the change of one vote would have taken the county seat from Sherman. A supervisor was approached with an offer of $10.00 if he would vote with Cadillac. The supervisor agreed to the deal and took the ten. When the roll was called at the next meeting, he told what had happened and named the supervisor who had given him the bribe. There was talk of arrests and bribery but nothing came of it.

Again, $300 was offered a Sherman supervisor. He was promised that his farm would be purchased at a good price and a house and lot secured for him in Clam Lake if he would favor the southern faction. He was also to be furnished protection from violence after he voted. In an unguarded moment, the supervisor told the wrong person who, in turn, told the county clerk, and the deal fell through.

For a number of years, there was bitterness between the people of Cadillac and the people in the northern part of the county.

As years have passed, however, residents in all parts of the county have come to realize that the Cadillac location of the county seat was the logical one. Its location is convenient for the majority of people in the county. It is rarely, indeed, that the broken noses, bruised knuckles, and injured feelings of the bygone struggle are remembered.

The old sidewalks in Sherman are overgrown with sod and the jail has rotted to the ground. The courthouse, used for a school for some time, was razed, and three fires, the last one in 1912, removed all of the business places.

It can be said that no village ever fought harder to live. Not until 1912, when the *Sherman Pioneer* issued its last paper with the headline "Last Visit," could she be called dead.

Wexford—The Ghost of a Ghost Town

IN 1871, at a regular meeting of the Board of Supervisors of Wexford County, it was resolved to do something about the sale of intoxicating beverages. To that end, the members of the board voted unanimously to "pledge ourselves to give aid and support to the . . . officers . . . whose duty it is to bring to justice all who may be found engaged in this wicked and unholy business."

Inasmuch as Wexford County has its center of population near the Grand Traverse County line at a point close to the present M-37, Traverse City papers made much of the fact that there would be a war on saloon owners.

Nothing ever came of the resolution, however, and shortly thereafter the little village of Wexford was organized and two of the early business places were saloons. Wexford was on the county line and the saloons were in Grand Traverse County, out of reach of the Carrie Nation politicians.

On present day standards, Wexford wasn't much shakes as a town. But on January 8, 1872, when J. Foust was appointed postmaster, it was the hub of a busy community life. Foust, who had been around the country looking for a likely place to settle, had been a coal miner in Ohio and had done considerable farming. He arrived in Grant Township, Grand Traverse County, in 1871. The village of Wexford was beginning to take shape, and, while Foust wasn't the first postmaster, he was appointed at a time when the future of the village looked pretty rosy.

Today Wexford is not even a ghost town. Nearly all of the homes and the long row of buildings which housed prosperous business ventures are gone. The spacious Gurnsey home, for instance, has been torn down, as has the old boarding house at the opposite end of the village. The little church was moved away and now serves its intended purpose at the village of Buckley, but there was a time when Wexford was a real place. A few of the old timers are still living who remember Doc Connine (D. W. Connine) and his bank, drug store and general store. John Lennington, who was really the founder of the town, had a general store, and J. Foust ran a store in connection with his postoffice operation. There was a nice hotel just south of the main corners, on the east side of the road. It was run by Andrew Ahl first and later sold to Elon Cornell, who, in turn, sold it to William Sheriff. The stone steps still remain but the building was torn down about a quarter of a century ago.

Ed Blackhurst was the blacksmith. Later he went into a mercantile business with Ed Connine, son of Dr. D. W. Connine. And Frank Benyou operated a barbershop near the bank.

There were two saloons during most of the time that Wexford lived. Merchants in the village complained that the rivermen and lumberjacks would cash their checks on payday in the saloons, both in Wexford and the nearby village of Sherman, in order to keep their credit good and then spend the remainder for groceries—sometimes not much.

William Sanford operated a confectionery and sold ice cream, and his wife did millinery work. Jim Hickey had a meat market and did a thriving business, especially about the time John Kennedy rounded up his crew and started out on his threshing tour.

Earl Cook, one of a large family of Cooks, operated a tin shop and did a booming business for several years. Andrew Ahl ran a stage line between Wexford and Grawn. There was also a stage line between Wexford and Mesick for a number of years. This was operated by Lon Hopkins.

The school house, at one time having all eight grades and enrolling as many as sixty youngsters, was located east of the village. As the neighboring Buckley community grew, the need for the school was lessened and it was ultimately razed.

It was in 1909 that a portion of the village burned. When the flames were first discovered, they had such a start that there wasn't much that could be done to save the village. Several stores and offices which were centrally located near the corners were burned to the ground. Old timers say that the blaze started in a back room in the Connine general store.

The overall picture of Wexford offers a note of surprise that it should have disappeared. It was in a progressive and prosperous farming area. It had a head start on any other village in the region. Its main street was nearly a quarter of a mile long and lined with prosperous business places.

True, it was off the beaten path and the Ann Arbor railway bypassed the village when it was surveyed through. Some of the old-timers feel that the influence of two or three residents of Wexford was responsible for the failure of the rails to hit the settlement. The coming of the rails, those men said, might spoil their business by making it easier for residents to go out of town to do their shopping.

After the disastrous fire, Connine rebuilt immediately in cement. Other business places were rebuilt and the village seemed to have recovered from the blow.

Such was not the case. First one family and then another moved away. Business became bad for the merchants and they, one by one, closed their doors. The Connine bank was no different. It closed. That was the telling blow for the village.

A drive through the village site today is well worthwhile. The old cement vault from the Connine bank still stands as it did at the turn of the century. The cement walls of such buildings as the Martin Stack Saloon, Dr. Purdy's Drug Store, the boarding house and many others are still there. Basements are being filled and grass has overgrown the old paths. Along the road there are still the cement sidewalks and the foundation of the Connine home remains sound enough to support a modern home.

Where the Wexford Hardware Company once operated there is a blacksmith shop and a car and tractor repair place operated by Hynec Svec. It is the only business still alive where there was once a bustling village.

Wexford remains only in the memories of the older folks. It is, today, only the ghost of a ghost town.

There'll Always be Kalkaska

IN THE beginning, insofar as the white man is concerned, the Kalkaska plateau was heavily timbered with the finest birch, beech, maple and pine timber to be found anywhere in the state. It was this timber which brought the first settlers to Kalkaska County and created an ultimate prosperity, a prosperity which has had its ups and downs over the past three quarters of a century.

Originally Kalkaska County received its name from a Pottawatomie chieftain who signed a treaty in 1821. In the early days, the area was called "Wabassee," meaning swan. In a state act of 1843, the county name was spelled Kalcasca. Later, it became Kalkaska. If the final naming is of Indian origin, as some think, it is probably a corruption of a Chippewa word meaning burned-over.

It was a hundred years ago that the first white settler located in the county. William Copeland, coming from the southern part of Michigan, took residence in Clear Water Township near the Grand Traverse County line. For twelve years Copeland and his wife were the only residents of Kalkaska County.

It was about the time of the Copeland arrival that a small dam was built at what later became known as Barker Creek. No extensive settlement was established at the dam.

The first organized township in the county was Rapid River. There were a few scattered residents in the county by 1868, and a very hot election campaign was going on in the young nation. General U. S. Grant was a candidate for the Presidency and the patriotic folks in Kalkaska wanted to cast their ballots. This could only be done if there was some place to vote. Norman Ross circulated a petition to form the village of Rapid River.

At one time, the county was attached to Grand Traverse County and later to Antrim. It remained attached to Antrim County until 1871 when it became a separate political unit. From 1871 on, for several years, Crawford County, then unorganized, was a part of Kalkaska County. The first meeting of the county Board of Supervisors was held in a school house known as the Round Lake School. The meeting was attended by A. T. Kellogg, H. U. Hill and A. W. Jones. A makeshift courthouse was erected in 1873; it was replaced in 1883.

In 1872, A. A. Abbott, Decatur, Michigan, decided to locate a mill at the present site of Kalkaska village, because he thought it would be the logical site for a county seat, being in line with the coming railway and centrally located. He bought a thousand acres of land from the railroad, Dexter and Noble and from Hannah, Lay and Company and built a mill on the north branch of Boardman River. From that time, the Abbott name was important to the county. It was the Abbott purchase and platting that established the village.

In the spring of 1873, a number of new families made their appearance in the village. Log houses were erected, a rooming house went into operation and the inevitable saloons opened. There were five of them.

In the same year, the Congregational Church established the first regular services. The influence of the church must have been good because records show that there began a decline in the saloon trade.

The first official school district was also organized in that year, and a frame school building was completed and opened in 1874. In 1884, a new union school was completed.

In 1887, Kalkaska was incorporated as a village. At that time, it boasted a considerable amount of industry. For example, there was a canthook factory. (A Kalkaska canthook was a good canthook.) A cement brick factory turned out countless thousands of bricks. A number of buildings still stand which were constructed of this brick. There was a sawmill and a gristmill and other minor industry.

A heretofore unheralded product of the county, one that brought thousands of dollars to early residents, was ginseng roots. The supply, however, was quickly exhausted, and now there is only an occasional plant to be found in the woods and no market for that.

Today, Kalkaska is a thriving village that is known across the Middle West. It has a smattering of modern industry and sound banking. There are churches and modern schools. Many of its streets are paved. It has a weekly newspaper which began as the *Kalkaskian* way back in 1874. Later, the *Kalkaska Leader* was published and, in 1911, the two papers merged as the *Kalkaskian-Leader*. J. N. Tinklepaugh was the manager of the consolidation. There is a good courthouse in the county seat and the main street boasts many modern shopping places.

A trout fishing celebration takes place each spring and guests at that time come from all over the Middle West. Winter sports are being looked upon as a new industry and a study is being made of the possibilities of a municipal ski area, though there already is a privately owned one open to public use and that has excellent patronage.

This, in a few words, is the story of Kalkaska County. Its dairying and other agricultural enterprises, its fruit farming and its oil wells are sidelights to the story.

Rip-Roaring South Boardman

THE VILLAGE of South Boardman, just off U. S. Route 131 in Kalkaska County and near the village of Fife Lake, has a population of one hundred and seventy-seven persons over the age of ten. That was the count on January 1, 1957. On May 12, 1903, the population was near fifteen hundred. It was a bustling lumber town.

A series of fires and then, in 1921, the "Big Fire," all but wiped the little place off the Michigan map. The big Anderson sawmill, the hotel, the postoffice, the restaurant, three stores and many other buildings went up in flames.

Rev. Alvin Ellis recalled that when he came to South Boardman in 1902 there were four churches and five saloons in the village. It was a rip-roaring lumber town and the "Big Mill" cut from ninety thousand to one hundred and twenty thousand feet of lumber every day. Main Street, which runs north and south, and Traverse Street, which runs east and west, were lined with shops and stores.

In 1921, a cigarette tossed from a window of a Main Street pool room did the trick. The next morning the village was a smouldering ruin. It never recovered. A gradual exodus of the residents began. The hardwood was gone and the mills were out.

A general store now operates on Main Street and there is one on Traverse Street. There is a tiny postoffice with twenty-six boxes, all rented but one. The postmaster, Lorna G. Lisch, has been at her post "a lot of years." She was born and raised in the community and knows its troubles and its prides.

The village got its name from the fact that it is located on the south branch of the Boardman River. The stream has its beginning about two or three miles above the town where a dozen or more little springs bubble from the hills and run together. At the village, the river reaches sufficient size to fill a pond to operate a small turbine sawmill, one of the very few such mills left in the Middle West.

Residents believe that there will always be a South Boardman and there is little reason to disagree with them. Now and then a new home is built to replace one which has been razed by man or the elements. U. S. Route 131, which skirts the town, has attracted a garage and gasoline station on one approach and a similar business with a restaurant on the other entrance.

When traffic swirls by at breakneck speed, South Boardman and its handful of people move along at an even pace conducive to peace of mind and rest of body.

France Has Fallen

FRANCE is no more. She has fallen, and where she stood are scores of wild apple trees, decayed foundations and overgrown roads and paths.

France, a village, later French Landing, was another of those fabulous sawmill towns which flourished during the late nineteenth century and early in the present one. It was located on the Pere Marquette Railroad, now the Chesapeake and Ohio, about four miles southwest of the village of Rapid City. At that time the area was known as the Round Lake Swamp and could be reached only by leaving the Rapid City road and following a private road into the slash area.

Round Lake Swamp produced thousands of giant telegraph poles, beautiful cedar lumber by the trainload, hardwood timber in vast quantities, and railroad ties.

The early history of France is somewhat vague. The property on which it stood was originally owned by a man named McNulty, who lived in Chicago. A conservationist and nature lover, McNulty had planned to make some sort of game refuge of the property, but his plans went awry somewhere along the line. He went so far as to build a nice home on a hill just west of Waldron Springs, and its ruins still are witness to his early plans.

The next owner of the timber rights was Link Simmons. The dense cedar timber in the swamp area was ideal for the location of a shingle mill. This mill was located, as near as can be determined by information available and by a close study of the site, at a point only a few rods southeast of a cabin now owned by Steve Davis of Traverse City. The mill employed about twenty-five hands. Mrs. Simmons operated a boarding house. The Simmons family erected a large log home on the hill overlooking a little creek, Chaney Creek, and its rotted foundation timbers, bits of broken crockery and worn paths can still be seen.

While Simmons operated his shingle mill, the French Lumber Company of Battle Creek came into the picture. It was primarily interested in the hardwood and pine holdings on the McNulty property. The French Company built a large sawmill, steam powered. At its peak it could cut ten thousand board feet of lumber a day.

The French mill gave the settlement its name. It was known all over the region as France. Not located on water suitable for logging operations, the company constructed an artifical soup hole for washing logs and floating them to the saw carriage. An excavation was made between the old shingle mill and the Pere Marquette tracks and was used as a backwater retainer. The soup hole is still there, grown to cattails and fast filling up with dead vegetation. It is not known how the excavation was filled with water. One old resident of the region said it was seepage water and another said the company had a large well, powered by the engine which ran the mill. A two-inch casing still is visible a few feet from the hole, lending weight to the possibility that some pumping was done. Nevertheless, it might have been a combination of the two methods. The big boiler still stands just a few feet from the east end of the soup hole. The footings and a large retaining wall of concrete remain in the swamp, only a few feet from the road to the Davis cabin.

It was about a half century ago that the French Lumber Company and the Simmons shingle mill operated. The railroad siding which served the two plants is no longer in evidence but the grade still shows. The siding was used as a wood shipping point and gave rise to the name of French Landing.

The old logging trails across the hills to the hardwood are no longer passable and the bridge over Chaney Creek is gone. In place of the bridge there is a sprawling beaver dam which, at times, creates a considerable backwater through the swamp.

One old building still retains a semblance of shape although over the decades it has fallen to ruin and only a few boards hang to each other, held by rusted nails and gravity. Prosperity clung to the location only a short time after the removal of the French mill.

The Elk Rapids Cement Plant

BUILDING material used in the construction of many of the business buildings in Traverse City, and in many of the foundations of the homes all over this region, has come from the bottom of the Petobego Swamp, north of Acme on U. S. Route 31. In fact, for a period of about ten years, the swamp provided employment for at least one hundred and twenty-five men around the clock.

The Elk Rapids Cement Company, a stock concern, was organized in 1899 and residents of the Elk Rapids community recall that it was about 1901 that the first commercial cement was produced. Just why it was originally decided to build on the shore of Grand Traverse Bay at the village of Elk Rapids is not positively known. With the raw materials coming from a distance of about three miles by tramcar, and a major portion of the finished product being shipped out by rail, it would seem more logical that the plant be located on the shores of the swamp. However, it was not the location of the industry which caused its downfall. It was progress. Competitive plants replaced the old German wet process of manufacture with the dry or kiln process, which was more economical in the long run. The Elk Rapids plant followed suit. The dry process entailed the shipping in of lime, gypsum, clay and shale. This material came from northern points and was expensive as well as time-taking. The dry materials were blended and fused by a coal dust blast and then ground to cement. The finished product was bagged and loaded onto rail cars for shipping on a spur track which cut across through a point about where the Elk Rapids municipal park is now located. The tram rails from the Petobego Swamp followed the bay shore for about two and a half miles and then cut across the present site of U. S. Route 31 to the swamp. Barges with steam-powered scoops dredged the marl from the bottom and loaded it onto the cars. An old engine from an eastern railway was secured to operate the short line.

The wages paid at the cement plant were nothing to write home about, although, in that day, they were a going figure. A twelve-hour day in the plant paid a total of $1.98. This was for such jobs as filling hoppers, loading clay and similar labor. Mechanics and skilled men got a little more per day. One shift went to work at 6 p.m. and quit at 6 a.m., when the second shift started. At the peak of its production the industry operated seven days a week. During the periods when the marl arrived from the swamp in larger quantities than the mill could use, it was dumped at the north end of the plant. Close examination of the earth in this area still reveals residual marl.

The old cement plant property has been cut up in "meets and bounds" descriptions and sold for resort cottages and permanent homes. Concrete foundations and drives are rapidly becoming a part of the landscape, and it is only a matter of time when the eyesore of another year will be one of the most beautiful spots on the bay.

At Petobego Swamp, earlier called Petobego Lake, can be seen the area excavated by the project. It is about the only part of the marsh not totally covered with swamp grass and reeds.

The cement plant was one of several enterprises in the Elk Rapids community which led residents to believe that, some day, they would have an industrial center second to none in the state. The lumber, the cement, the iron, and the flour mills, and other enterprises, made a strong bid to make this a reality. Though the boom failed to carry through, Elk Rapids never lost its will to do and its enterprising outlook. Today, though not a metropolis, it is a thriving resort town, and it also has the beginning of a new lease on industrial life.

The Iron Rule

THERE IS little doubt that the largest industrial concentration ever to hit northern Michigan was the Dexter and Noble plant at Elk Rapids, flourishing before the turn of the century. Even the giant sawmill of Perry Hannah and A. Tracy Lay, located in Traverse City, could not compare with the scope and production of the Elk Rapids concern.

It all began in 1855 when Henry H. Noble arrived in the then sprawling lumbering town of Elk Rapids. He accepted a position with the M. Craw Company, manufacturers of lumber. Soon after that, the firm of Dexter and Noble was organized and a great expansion began. In 1865, Edwin S. Noble, a giant in mind and muscle, joined the firm.

Before the end of Edwin Noble's career, the company produced thousands of tons of high grade pig iron, countless barrels of wood alcohol, tar and tar products, acetate of lime for the manufacture of acetic acid, charcoal in such quantities that it was never estimated, and carloads of high grade wheat flour, and, on the side, it operated a general store that was, at that time, compared with Chicago's great Marshall Field store.

The Elk Rapids Iron Company, a Dexter and Noble enterprise, was started in 1882 and was known locally as the "blast furnace." Three years later the first export of its charcoal pig iron was shipped out of New York, bound for England. Not only was this the first export from the Elk Rapids furnace, but it is also believed to have been the first from the United States.

The magnitude of the Elk Rapids Iron Company can be imagined when a survey of their holdings is reviewed.

In 1887, it was estimated that there would be enough wood on the Dexter and Noble holdings to last thirty-five years if the furnaces used one hundred and fifty cords daily. Using the estimated available wood along the shores of the Chain of Lakes, the firm leaders believed the plant would operate for another half century.

The Dexter and Noble holdings in the Elk Rapids area, which included a blast furnace, charcoal kilns and chemical works, where wood alcohol and tar products were produced. Elk Lake is in the background.

The sawmill was capable of turning out sixty thousand board feet of lumber daily and the planer could turn out a total of seventy-five thousand board feet of dressed lumber. The flour mill could grind and process a hundred barrels of flour daily.

The blast furnace was topped by a forty-eight foot cupola and the base of the tower measured ten feet in diameter. Charcoal, lime and ore were hoisted to the top of the tower by conveyor elevator. A blast used seventeen hundred pounds of ore, forty bushels of charcoal, and 20 per cent lime.

There were at one time thirty-five charcoal kilns, each capable of holding a hundred cords of four-foot wood. It took four to five days to burn a kiln and from seven to ten days for the charcoal to cool so that it could be removed. Of this charcoal, the blast furnace burned over five thousand bushels daily.

The firm owned and operated twenty-four scows and three tugs, used to haul the timber down from the Chain of Lakes. There is no accurate record of the number of men employed in the woods, but it is known that the payroll of

Dexter and Noble, even with the low wage of that era, would be a welcome addition to the economy of any community today.

The chemical plant, associated with the furnace, produced as much as ninety thousand gallons of 80 per cent wood alcohol daily. The unrefined crude chemical poured from the plant at a rate of ten to twenty-five gallons a minute after distillation had been completed. The alcohol distilling plant used five great tanks, fifteen thousand gallons each, in which to store the raw stock and from the residual tank came approximately twelve barrels of tar daily.

The blast furnace turned out about sixteen thousand tons of pigs annually and the payroll at the furnace and the kilns was one hundred and sixty men. A quarter of a million dollars was the annual cost of labor and products combined, and this included four-foot wood at $1.25 a cord.

Using wheat grown by the residents of the community, the mill turned out $50,000 worth of flour the first year of operation. The flour, made from winter wheat, was called Noble flour after one of the partners in the firm and was shipped all over the Middle West.

The general store was a cash and carry enterprise. The store paid cash and demanded cash for merchandise. If a farmer brought in a load of wood or a load of potatoes he was paid at the cashier's cage and could spend his money in any manner he chose. There was never a company store, where workman or vendor was paid in script or token. It was hard cash both ways for Dexter and Noble.

Iron from the furnace was shipped from the Elk Rapids dock to Chicago and Milwaukee by ship, until the coming of the rails in 1890, near the end of the flourishing life of the enterprise.

Visualize, if you can, a sawmill capable of cutting twelve million feet of lumber annually, a giant blast furnace sending pig iron across the nation, chemical retorts producing alcohol in a flow that would shame a modern plant, a flour mill capable of furnishing enough of its product for a community twenty times the size of Elk Rapids. Then picture a general store with a stock inventoried at $100,000 at the low prices of a half century ago. All this in a village of six hundred people.

While the holdings of the Hannah and Lay Company in the Traverse City area were known as the H. and L. "dukedom," the Dexter and Noble holdings were known as a "principality."

Local people who wish to make a drive to Elk Rapids today will see the remains of the old blast furnace. The cement foundations are on the right side of the new bridge where the highway joins U.S. Route 31. It will pay well to stop and walk over the ruins. On a ridge of earth which extends away from the blast furnace foundation will be seen countless pieces of colorful slag. This glassy substance, a refuse item from the furnace, is green, black, gray and brown and has the sheen of obsidian. Across the highway from the ruins were the charcoal kilns, a boarding house and many other buildings.

Some day the old concrete foundations will probably be blasted and removed to make way for progress, and another landmark will live only in the memories of the very old people of the region.

A "wannigan" or "wangan," which was a floating bunkhouse and cook shack. It was used when lumbering operations were conducted near large bodies of water. This "wannigan" belonged to the Dexter and Noble company of Elk Rapids. In the foreground is cordwood slated for the Dexter and Noble blast furnace and chemical plant near Elk Rapids.

A Landmark Must Go

IN MAY 1957, at the regular meeting of the Board of Supervisors of Antrim County, the death knell was sounded for one of the most popular tourist attractions in the state of Michigan, a landmark that stood as a monument to the spirit of the pioneers for more than a half century. It was during this session that the board voted to approve the construction of a fixed bridge over Clam River, at Clam River village, Antrim County, eliminating the old hand-operated swing bridge which had given a half century of service. The new bridge, with a proposed clearance of thirteen feet above the level of the river, is to be located only a short distance up-river from the present old landmark.

How did the Clam River community react to the decision of the engineers and the approval of the board? Of the many people contacted with a direct query regarding the replacement of the old bridge, most of them were against it.

Engineers' figures backed the decision of the supervisors to replace the bridge. The old structure, they claimed, was a traffic hazard in the matter of tonnage passing over it. Designed to support ten tons, the bridge was handling traffic which should have passed over a bridge designed for twenty tons. Too, the engineers pointed out, the bridge was opened four hundred and five times in a single year at an operating cost which was not favorable to maintaining its existence.

Residents of the region, however, felt that the number of times the bridge was opened in a year was of less importance than the hundreds of guests who drove many miles just to take pictures of the old bridge and to drive over it. They were flat in their statement that it was one of the major tourist attractions in the north.

The Clam River swing bridge is one of the two such gateways on the famous Chain of Lakes.

Another, although less colorful, is located at the village of Torch River. This structure was recently mechanized, leaving the one at Clam River village alone in its field.

Before the construction of the swing bridge over Clam River, shortly after the turn of the century, there was a "barge bridge" to provide a crossing. According to old-timers in the area, Dexter and Noble, owners of an empire of timber lands and operators of mills and a smelter at Elk Rapids, placed one of their scows across the river. Boat passage was permitted by pulling the bridge upstream until the craft had passed and then allowing the bridge to float back into position.

Several versions of how the first bridge was operated have been given. One old-timer states that it was pulled around with a horse. Another emphatically declares that it was hauled by manpower. Handpower, horsepower, it makes little difference today. Sufficient to know that there was passage over the river as early as 1875.

There was always the question as to the need of a swing bridge with high clearance on the Chain of Lakes route. When the facts are made clear, statistics studied, there remains little doubt about the popularity of the narrows at Clam River as a boat passage.

The earliest steam-power boat on the Chain of Lakes, as far as can be determined, was the *Jennie Silkman* which was owned and operated by Silkman and Hart, pioneer lumbermen at Torch Lake, earlier known as Brownstown. Another craft, built to assist in the log rafting operating on the lakes was the *Mud Hen*. This latter boat was originally named the *Grass Lake* but acquired the less glamorous name from lumberjacks and millhands.

One of the major users of the Chain of Lakes and, of course, the swing bridge, was the Dexter and Noble firm at Elk Rapids. The *Queen of the Lakes*, a passenger and freight steamer, was the first boat to pass through the swing bridge after it was completed about 1907. She was a side-wheeler, as was the *City of Cheboygan*, another craft which plied the Chain.

Other ships and tugs in the Dexter and Noble fleet were the *Albatross*, the *Lake Erie* and a number of scows and barges which made regular trips around the lakes. Also, there are memories of the *Odd Fellow* and the *Mable*, which was originally named the *Bellaire*.

A Captain Hall once guided a broad-beamed boat named the *Times* around the banks and through the narrows of the rivers and lakes. Then, there was the *Maple Leaf* and the *Annie S.* After the early and clumsy lumbering craft came the sleek *Lizzie Rose* which carried both passengers and freight to lake ports.

The steamer Topinabee which conducted a ferry service on the Inland Route. It is shown here rounding The Devil's Elbow on the crooked river with, apparently, a boat-load of Sunday excursionists.

Sailing the Chain of Lakes was not a job for an apprentice. It was a trade which only years of work and hardship could teach. The pilots knew where every shallows was located, where every mud flat projected and where the current built its channels.

So difficult was the going over some of the stretches of river that the passengers on loaded boats were required at times to go aft to raise the bow and then rush forward to raise the stern while the propellors churned through the sand bars and flats.

Today, there is a vast change in the use of the river on the Chain. Where land was of no use other than for the timber it supported seventy-five years ago, it is now valued highly as resort property. Almost every resort owner has some sort of boat, many of them sailing craft with auxiliary power. To move from one of the lakes to another requires passage through the Clam River bridge or the narrows at Torch Lake village.

To properly envision the magnitude of the area affected by water transportation on the Chain of Lakes, it is necessary to know the extent of the water involved and the miles one can travel without getting ashore.

The Chain, of course, starts at Elk Rapids with Elk Lake, which is six miles long. Then there are Torch Lake with a length of eighteen miles, Central Lake with a length of about two miles and Intermediate Lake which is just short of five miles in length. Clam Lake, into which empties Clam River, has a length of a little less than four miles while Grass Lake is just over four miles long. In all, there are over one hundred and fifty miles of shoreline on the Chain of Lakes.

It is estimated that about fifty sailboats, having auxiliary power, will be unable to use the proposed new bridge. On the other hand, boats over twenty-five feet in length have serious difficulty in negotiating the Chain because of the limiting size of Grass River, connecting link between Clam Lake and Grass Lake.

It would seem, to the casual observer, that the removal of the old hand-operated swing bridge at Clam River village is an esthetic problem. The old-timers can recall when it was the gateway to their outposts and as such they still envision it. They remember when rafts of pine moved down Clam River to Elk Rapids as a cash crop; sound birch logs and number one basswood bringing $3.00 a thousand feet when skidded to the banks of lakes or rivers. They remember the steamers which made the course, bringing supplies and mail. Those boats, and their hardy crews, were not for pleasure but, rather, they were the connecting link between the lumber camps and another world.

Frank Lyon, a pioneer in the Clam Lake area, is one of the old-timers who recalled the rise and decline of the Chain of Lakes traffic. He saw the coming of the rails and the disappearance of the shallow draft tugs and passenger boats.

Frank, at one time a licensed engineer on all inland Michigan waters, rode the *Hattie Kay* when she made the tortuous course from Elk Rapids to the head of the Chain. He resented the thought of the old swing bridge at Clam River giving way to a modern giant of cement and steel. Without the old landmark, the course won't be the same.

It has been many years now since a steamer has chugged through the inland passage. The belching smoke of pitch pine slabs and hardwood chunks is gone. The virgin forests are also history.

But, there are memories. To the pioneers who still remain, those memories will retain their usual brilliance once the squeaking and weathered bridges give way to progress. And give way they must. They have held on tenaciously to the ways of another era, which is now a memory. But modern, heavy traffic cannot move on memories.

The Saga of the Passenger Pigeon

ONLY NOW and then can we find a person who can remember the fantastic era of the wild passenger pigeon in the Grand Traverse region and its ultimate extinction.

When the last known of the species died in captivity on September 1, 1914, there was a hue and cry about the "meat-hunters" having been at fault. No one ever argued the fact that the hoards of trappers and hunters contributed to the extinction of the bird. However, study and understanding of nature's balance brings to light a number of other reasons why the pigeon disappeared.

The story of the birds as they roared over Grand Traverse County and the counties to the north is almost unbelievable. Tales of how the flocks darkened the sky, of how hunters and trappers swarmed into the region to make their fortunes, and of how Indians shot the squabs from their nests with blunt arrows, may tax the imagination.

It is true that the harvest of passenger pigeons reached fantastic proportions. By boat and by freight car, the birds were shipped to metropolitan markets. They were served in cafes, hotels and restaurants, and, costing only four or five cents each, they provided an economy menu.

The flesh of the adult pigeon was dark, much like that of a guinea fowl, while that of the young birds was much lighter and usually very fat. The squabs, when pushed from their nests at about the age of three weeks, were nearly as heavy as the parent birds.

In flight, the pigeons were blue-gray in color with an iridescent breast of gold, purple and gray. From wing-tip to wing-tip they measured about fifteen inches; when on the ground or in a tree, they were about the size of the common mourning dove.

While they had favorite nesting and feeding grounds all over the Grand Traverse region, they seemed to follow a pattern. In the Traverse City area their route followed the east shore of west Grand Traverse Bay. Between Petoskey and Charlevoix there was a fly-way which was equally as trafficked as the one in Traverse City, and one was followed at Frankfort by flocks so immense that they reportedly darkened the sun.

The pigeons, coming in in the evening from their feeding grounds, would be so low that they could be clubbed from the air. Mark Craw, only a tad of a boy during the great flights and now residing at Birchwood on the east side of Traverse City, remembers well the millions of pigeons which came in the evening and left in the morning:

"When they came in at night they seemed to be tired. They were flying low and their wingbeat was not like it would be at other times.

"I remember how the men used to congregate near the bay, on what is now Elmwood Avenue, to shoot. Malcolm Winnie lived on the road and I remember well because there was an unidentified grave on his property. The men stood along the road in front of the Winnie property and shot the pigeons as they headed for their nesting grounds along Franke Creek, headwaters of Asylum Creek.

"No one cared about who shot which bird as there was plenty of game and not many shotguns.

"Kids weren't really welcome at the shoots, but I remember one time the men ran low on shot. They chipped in and got enough money to buy twenty-five pounds. I ran all the way to the Hannah, Lay and Company store and got the bag of shot and got back as fast as I could."

Mrs. Frances Youmans, now living just south of Traverse City, recalled, on her hundredth birthday, that she earned spending money when she was in her teens by picking pigeons. She described the process in this manner:

"We picked the feathers dry and took off the heads and wings; the birds were then packed in barrels with ice and evergreen boughs and hauled to the shipping center where they were loaded in railway cars and delivered to the big cities."

The nesting grounds on Franke Creek was an area known as the Elm Flats. The entire area, now occupied by Brookside Subdivision and the state hospital property, as far south as Oleson's fish pond was a dense stand of tall elm trees.

The pigeons built as many as twenty to thirty nests in the branches. The nests were crude flat structures of coarse sticks and contained sometimes two, but more often a single baby bird.

Because of the necessity of foraging far for food with which to support the family the parents each contributed to the effort. Squabs became rolling fat from this doting attention. Just before they were fully feathered and able to fly, the parents gently nudged them from the nest and they went fluttering to the ground. The squabs were in much the same position as the ancient dodo. They were fat and heavy and could only flutter along the ground, easy prey for men, women and children.

When the flights were at their peak, say the old-timers who remember, the flocks were so dense that hunters without firearms would throw sticks into the flocks, swing pieces of lumber, even stones, and get birds.

Netters, the commercial men who filtered into the area, took tons of pigeons. Their nets, woven in square mesh not unlike a fisherman's net, were set on spring poles with trigger ropes. As many as three hundred to five hundred birds were often taken with a single baited trap.

Live pigeons were in great demand and brought premium prices. They were shipped, in wicker and wire cages and sometimes in crude crates made from mill edgings, to sporting clubs in all parts of the Middle West and in the east. They were released one at a time as targets for marksmen and were the forerunners of the clay pigeon of today.

The greatest recorded migrations were in the years between 1875 and 1885. An oddity of the day is the fact that regional newspapers made little or no mention of the phenomenal flight of passenger pigeons.

On March 28, 1878, the *Grand Traverse Herald* carried this very short statement, printed in 8-point type on an inside page:

"There is an immense pigeon roost about halfway between Charlevoix and Petoskey.

"Myriads of pigeons are nesting in that vicinity and the air is darkened with them at times."

Again, on May 9, 1878, there was this terse mention of the pigeons:

"A few pigeons are left near Petoskey. Three to six tons are being shipped south every day."

149

Then, until 1881, there was no mention of the birds. A cat belonging to M. V. B. Clark caught a pigeon, indicating that the flocks were on the wane in this area.

Financially, the birds never meant much to the region. They were a source of quick money for a few people, like the berry harvest. The birds brought from twenty-five cents to thirty-five cents a dozen packed in ice and from a dollar to two dollars crated alive. The major money, of course, was made by the commercial trappers who came with extensive equipment. They hired women and children to assist in the dressing and packing.

A major portion of the consignments out of Traverse City were shipped by boat. The *City of Traverse*, on schedule between Chicago and the north, got the lion's share of the business. A heavy traffic was also carried by the Grand Rapids and Indiana Railway and, at times, the depot was almost dwarfed by the double decked cages awaiting transportation.

Fantastic as the stories seem, most of them are true. The pigeons were in the area in numbers that almost defy the imagination. It is true that they were also in most of the central and eastern states, but they favored the Grand Traverse region as a nesting place and feeding grounds. The hardwoods of Wisconsin provided beechnuts and acorns for food and the trees provided a nesting haven.

During their peak they destroyed entire grain fields overnight. Vegetarian by nature, they devoured everything which looked like food.

Why are they gone? Conservationists cling to their belief that they were slaughtered out of existence. Those who have studied their life and disappearance reason otherwise. While admitting that the meat hunters contributed much to their extinction, they admit many other factors. Lack of food is one supposition. Slaughter, disease, starvation and their natural, massed-migration habits joined in the destruction.

BENEATH
FATHOMS
OF WATER

Even when fact and fiction are separated and the glitter of retold tales is shadowed, Captain Daniel Seavey remains one of the most rugged and roistering characters ever to sail the Great Lakes. Captain Dan, if even a portion of the tales is to be accepted, was a hard-fighting, hard-drinking skipper who . . .

Vessels of the Past

THERE IS an interesting contrast to the shipping facilities of 1899 with those of thirty years earlier. In 1851, and up to the time the Grand Rapids and Indiana Railroad reached Traverse City, Grand Traverse Bay and Lake Michigan were the only outlets to the outer world. The tonnage was trifling, with the exception of lumber which became a considerable product. The first vessel to carry freight for Hannah, Lay and Company and owned by them was the brig *J. Y. Scammon,* which was wrecked on the Manitous the first year of her service.

Their next ship was the schooner *Telegraph,* which served very well for three or four years prior to 1859. Then the firm bought the propeller ship *Allegheny,* the first steam vessel to ply the waters of the bay, with the exception of a vessel of the government land department. For service around the bay the firm built the small steamer *Sunnyside,* in 1864. She was wrecked at Charlevoix in 1867. Subsequently, for several years two other steamers ran on the bay, the *Ella Burrows,* captained by O. B. Burrows, and the *Ben H. E. Paine,* captained by J. W. Brown. Captain Brown was a pioneer of Torch Lake, and it was he who located the lands later owned by the Cameron Lumber Company. The small steamer *Clara Belle* was placed on the bay route in 1875 and was used for about ten years, when she was sold and went to Charlevoix. In 1879 the steamer *City of Grand Rapids* was put in commission, and the year following the *F. S. Saxon* was added. These boats did good service for Hannah, Lay and Company and helped to build up the small towns along the bay shores, affording frequent and direct transit to and from Traverse City.

The Traverse Bay Line of Steamers began business on the bay and lake in the late eighties. Captain H. J. Webb bought a half interest in the steamer

Onekama in 1887 from Manistee parties, the remaining interest being owned by Captain J. U. Emory. In 1888 they bought the *Lou A. Cummings* and put her on the East Jordan run. Captain Webb took control of the Bay Line in 1890 and bought the *Crescent*. In 1892, he had the *Columbia* built. The *Onekama* was taken off the Bay Line and run separately to various lake points by Captain Emory, who had purchased Captain Webb's interest. The line did good business and gave excellent service on the bay, carrying passengers and freight to Omena, Northport, Ne-ah-ta-wanta, and Suttons Bay, being an important influence in developing the bay resorts.

The Herschel *of Chicago anchored off* The Weguetong Club, Traverse City, 1894. *With the aid of a magnifying glass one can see a member of the crew, apparently peering at the photographer from the stern.*

In 1898 the *Columbia* and *Crescent* were on the Northport route and the *Cummings* ran between Northport and Charlevoix. The *Columbia* and *Crescent* were popular as excursion boats and were well fitted for boats of their class. Captain Charles A. Webb commanded the *Columbia*, Captain George Johnson, the *Crescent*, and Captain H. C. Plummer, the *Cummings*.

The steamer *Illinois* plied Lake Michigan and Grand Traverse Bay and was a great contrast to the unpretentious vessels which carried lumber and passengers during the early days. She was the largest of her class on the lakes at the turn of the century and made two round trips a week from the opening to closing of navigation. On the same line, the Northern Michigan Transportation Company, the *City of Charlevoix* was on the regular Chicago and Mackinaw run, alternating trips with the *Illinois*. She was a fine boat for her day, but was less commodious than the *Illinois*. This line began business in the bay in 1880 with the steamers *Lawrence* and *Champlain* and ran two boats a week.

The *Illinois* was the fastest passenger and freight steamer on the bay. She could make eighteen miles an hour and was luxuriously appointed. She was two hundred and forty feet long and had a forty foot beam, easily carried two hundred and fifty passengers and fifteen hundred tons of freight, and had triple-expansion engines of fifteen hundred horse power and two boilers. She was of steel throughout and built on beautiful lines. Her cost was $250,000. Captain William Finucan was in command. Eventually the *Illinois* replaced the *Charlevoix* on the Chicago and Mackinaw run and the *Charlevoix* replaced the *Petoskey*, which was sold to the Hart Line of Green Bay.

The enterprise and progressive spirit of the Northern Michigan Transportation Company did a great deal toward building up Traverse City and in developing the summer retreats in the area, since it reached the numerous resorts around the bay.

The J. W. Wescott, a lumber schooner, at the Traverse City piers. It is loaded with unfinished pine bound for Chicago.

The Christmas Tree Ship

IF IT WOULD be possible to erect a marker on the rolling surface of Lake Michigan there would, certainly, be one somewhere off Kewaunee, Wisconsin, a monument to the *Rouse Simmons*, a doughty sailing craft, and all hands. She foundered in a bitter November storm in 1912. Lost with the crew and passengers were Captain Oscar Nelson and his beautiful wife. In all, sixteen lives were lost.

The story of the sailing of the *Rouse Simmons*, known up and down the coasts for nearly a half century as the "Christmas Tree Ship," is the story of many ships which braved the late sailing conditions on the Great Lakes.

She was under charter to Herman Schuenemann to carry a cargo of Christmas trees from the Manistique area to Chicago for the Yule trade. Her home port was St. James Bay on Beaver Island at a time when King James Strang was the powerful ruler of that tiny Mormon kingdom.

Scheunemann was a well-liked dealer in holiday evergreens at the Clark Street dock, Chicago, where he had regular customers. The business had been started by his brother, August, who went down in a storm in 1898. Following the death of August, Herman carried on the trade alone.

The *Rouse Simmons* sailed from Thompson, a tiny upper lakes port, on November 22, 1912. She weighed anchor in the teeth of a gale and with the thermometer far below freezing. The demanding trade in Chicago is believed to have been the reason for the unfavorable sailing.

First authentic report of the ill-fated craft after she sailed was just off Point Aux Barques when she was sighted by the tug *Burger* which was towing the ship *Dutch Boy*. At that time the *Rouse Simmons* was headed into the great expanse of open and rolling lake, her deck piled high with spruce and balsam trees.

The next reliable report of the ship was when she was sighted by a lookout at the Kewaunee life-saving station; that was on Saturday afternoon November 23. At that time, according to a story in the *Kewaunee Enterprise* of that date, she was too far away and the water too rough for an attempt to aid her despite the fact that she was flying distress signals. Efforts were made to send a tug to aid her but this was not possible. Soon after she was sighted, a heavy snow began to fall and the visibility was cut to zero. A telephone call from the Kewaunee station to the Two Rivers station to the south sent a power-boat out in search of the ship but the men returned about 5:30 without having sighted her.

That was the last time the *Rouse Simmons* was ever seen. A revenue cutter, *Tuscarora*, left Milwaukee to assist in the search but nothing ever came of it. In fact, a passing ship gave the skipper of the *Tuscarora* wrong information and the rescue ship sailed clear to Racine before it headed back. By that time the *Rouse Simmons* was deep under the lake surface.

Even a few years ago fishermen reported snagging spruce and balsam trees in their nets, believed to be the scattered cargo of the Christmas Tree Ship. The exact spot where the craft foundered is not known. The general locality was determined by the trees which came ashore in the November gale.

Later a corked bottle was picked up on the Wisconsin beach, in it was a note of the following text:

"Friday. Everybody goodbye. I guess we are all through. Sea washed over our deckload Thursday. During the night the small boat was washed over. Ingvald and Steve fell overboard Thursday. God help us. Herman Schuenemann."

Whether this message was authentic or not will never be known. Most sources say no.

However, in April 1924, a pocketbook was found in which there was a receipt bearing the still readable signature of Herman Schuenemann. This was authentic.

Another bottle containing a message was found in 1927, purporting to have been cast overboard by a member of the ill-fated crew. The message reads:

"These lines are written at 10:30 p.m. Schooner R. S. ready to go down about 20 miles off Two Rivers Point. All hands lashed to one line. Goodbye. Oscar Nelson."

As in the case of the other message, the authenticity of the note was never proved. It is very doubtful.

The tragic sinking of the Christmas Tree Ship did not end the activities of the Schuenemann family. The widow and two daughters carried on under the family name for nearly a quarter of a century. One of the daughters, Elsie Schuenemann Roberts, passed away in 1952.

The *Rouse Simmons* visited Grand Traverse harbors many times and there is no doubt but that many of the crew members were known to the old timers of the region.

Lost in the tragedy, in addition to Captain and Mrs. Nelson and Schuene-mann, were Alex Johnson, Edward Minoque, George Watson, Ray Davis, Grule Peterson, Edward Hogan, Conrad Griffen, George Quinn, Edward Murphy, John Morawauski, Stump Morris, Frank Paul and Phillip Bauswein. The last six had been engaged in cutting the trees and were returning with the ship.

(Much information for this story is from the files of Captain Art Frederick-son, Frankfort.)

Our Son, *Last of the Windjammers*

ONE OF THE most colorful ships ever to visit the Grand Traverse ports during the days of the timber moguls and roaring mills was *Our Son* of Milwaukee. She was a trim, barque-rigged windjammer carrying a foremast, mainmast and mizzen. She was built in 1875 by Captain Henry Kelly, who had his headquarters at Black River, Ohio, later Lorain.

The story of the *Our Son*, and there are plenty of local folks who remember her when she used to weigh anchor off Traverse City and head for the lower lake with a load of lumber or timbers, is probably one of the most colorful of any craft ever to sail the Great Lakes.

An interesting fact about her was the name she carried. She was named *Our Son* when she slid down the hemlock ways at Black River and, unlike most craft on the lakes, she never changed her name. Her naming was the result of a tragedy. It was a tribute and a monument to the son of Captain Henry Kelly, who fell from the half completed boat at Black River and was drowned.

Local folks who recall the *Our Son* are not able to state her specifications. To them she was just another of the scores of craft which visited the docks. From the records, she was 182.1 feet overall and had a beam of 35.1 feet. She was thirteen feet deep and could carry over one thousand tons of ore or forty thousand bushels of grain. Under full sail and with a fair breeze she could make as much as fifteen miles an hour, an unusually good speed for a ship of her 720 gross tons. She carried a crew of seven throughout her life.

She sank as she sailed, a windjammer, never having converted to steam, as so many of her sister and companion ships had done. For almost fifty-five years she drove before the winds on the Great Lakes and went down in a gale on

September 26, 1930. She was carrying a cargo of pulpwood and her grave is about twenty-five miles off the Sheboygan, Wisconsin, harbor. During her late life she was the only cargo ship under sail on Great Lakes waters.

Our Son, *a schooner out of Milwaukee; she was the last of the windjammers to sail the Great Lakes, and called often at ports in the Grand Traverse region.*

Her sinking is the story of the stoic hardiness of the men who manned the windjammers. Captain Fred Nelson was in command and the usual crew was aboard. The gale she was fighting increased in intensity off the Sheboygan shore and she began to fill. The accepted distress signal of all sailors, the national emblem upside down, was run up on the mizzenmast. The steamer *William Nelson*, under the command of Captain Charles Mohr, saw the signal and changed course. The *Pere Marquette No. 22*, under the command of W. H. Van Dyke, also came to the scene to assist. The *William Nelson* maneuvered two hours before an oil slick (storm oil) quieted the sea enough to remove the crew. Aboard the *Pere Marquette No. 22* was a camera enthusiast, a man named Ferris, who took the last photo ever made of the *Our Son.* Her bare masts were adorned with only the American flag, upside down. Her canvas lay torn on her deck.

The City of Traverse

THE *CITY OF TRAVERSE* was built in the shipyards of Quails and Martin, Cleveland, and launched on May 1, 1871, for Hannah, Lay and Company, Traverse City. The *Cleveland Plain Dealer*, comenting on the launching, said the craft was probably the best of her class on the Great Lakes.

She was 225 feet long with a beam of 32 feet, 9 inches. The main deckhouse was 90 feet long and 12 feet wide and had twenty-one state rooms. Her capacity load was 640,000 feet of lumber and seventy-five passengers, and a crew.

The original plan of the Hannah, Lay and Company was to run her on regular trips between Traverse City and Chicago, but the high cost of freight transportation forced them to deviate from their original plan and, during the first year afloat, she made four trips between Buffalo and Chicago and also stopped at Erie. She carried grain.

At the close of the first season her log showed thirty-three trips to Chicago in addition to four special voyages; she had carried over 12 million feet of lumber and nearly 250,000 bushels of grain. The purser listed 1,040 passengers, 592 into Traverse City and 448 out.

During her first season, she was under the command of Captain Charles Baldwin. Other officers were Mate Eli Coon, Second Mate John Snow, Steward S. E. Wait, Engineer David Bauld and Assistant Engineer William Bauld. In July, Wait was taken ill and was replaced by a cabin boy, Will W. Smith. Smith later served Traverse City as mayor for two terms and was, still later, elected to the state senate.

The fate of the *City of Traverse* was not a pleasant one. She was later sold to a group of Chicago individuals who hoped to evade the long arm of the law in the matter of handling race track results. She was rigged as a modern poolroom and anchored several miles off the shore of Chicago. Using wireless telegraph, which was then coming into its own, she operated thus for about two and a half years. For years she was used as a part of a dock back of the old depot at Benton Harbor. A few years ago she was dismantled, and today she lies buried and rotting in mud and silt at the head of a slip canal.

The appearance of the *City of Traverse* is described in the following transcription from the *Grand Traverse Herald* of May 4, 1871:

"This fine new steamer, arrived on Monday morning last. She was greeted by a large crowd of people who boarded and examined her with a high degree of satisfaction. We are confident, it is the unanimous verdict of our citizens that all that has been said in her favor was well deserved.

"On Monday afternoon David Bauld, engineer, under whose supervision the boat was built and furnished, politely showed us though the entire craft, pointing out and explaining to us many things of great interest.

"We shall not now attempt any general description of the *City of Traverse*. That has already been done in our columns in articles copied from other papers. But in looking through the boat, among the many commendable things which we noticed were some so admirable and so important that we cannot pass them over in silence.

"We never before examined a boat that appeared to be so strongly built. Mr. Bauld assured us that she is 'as strong as wood and iron can make her,' and, after looking through her we could not doubt his statement. All the material used is of the best quality. Everything is heavy, braced, barred, bolted, spiked and fastened as firmly in its place as the highest skill and the most abundant means could do.

"Next to the substantial character of the boat the fact that most strongly impressed us is the unusual precautions against fire. The fires and boilers are completely encased in iron. The room in which they are placed is iron above, below, and all around. So, too, every stove is not only fastened by screws in the usual way, but is secured by a rod passing over it and made fast to the deck. The lamps used are all of the nonexplosive kind. How many steamers have been set on fire by the upsetting of stoves or the bursting of lamps! Those dangers are effectually guarded against in this boat.

"Pumps, to be worked both by steam and by hand, are found in various parts of the boat. Water and steam can be applied almost instantaneously and in large quantities wherever it may be needed to extinguish fire.

"Another important point is the roomy character of the boat. Everywhere, in the cabins, in the state rooms, in the halls and passage ways, there is room.

"Finally, in all the arrangements and furnishings of the boat regard seems to have been had to the comfort, convenience and safety of her passengers. The cabins and state rooms are pleasant and commodious and as tastefully and richly furnished as the most fastidious could desire. The beds consist of excellent mattresses on the improved wire support. Such beds are said to be perfectly luxurious. Every state room is supplied with several of the best cork life preservers.

"The owners of the *City of Traverse* have reason to be proud of their new boat, and the people of the Traverse region may well congratulate themselves that they now really have a floating palace on which to make their trips to the 'outside world.' Mr. Bauld, under whose supervision, as before stated, everything has been done, has good reason to be proud of his winter's work. The owners were certainly fortunate in committing the charge of this important work to so competent and faithful a man.

"The new boat, in all its departments, will be in excellent hands. In addition to the officers heretofore announced, it gives us pleasure to state that Mr. S. E. Wait, of this village, well and favorably known to everybody in this region, is to officiate as clerk and steward. Mr. Wait will make an efficient and gentlemanly officer . . . ."

Tragedy on Lake Leelanau

JUST SOUTH of the village of Lake Leelanau, three miles along the shore road, lies the rotted old planking of a ship that made history on the inland waterway between the village of Leland and the village of Fouch, located on the southern tip of Lake Leelanau.

In the old planking and a semblance of oaken ribs lies all that remains of the *Leelanau*, a ship of splendid service and great tragedy. She has rotted on the spot where her last owner, seriously ill, ran her aground. He later died in the Traverse City Hospital without ever boarding her again.

The *Leelanau* was launched at Lake Leelanau in 1900. She was built by Louis Mosher, assisted by his sons, Leo and Joe. Her ribs were cooked in open-air kettles and bent to shape by hand. Her fittings, boiler and engine were taken from an old ship, the *Ransom Brothers*, which had been secured from the Leland Iron Company. Prior to that, the *Ransom Brothers* had been brought around the Great Lakes from Buffalo, where she had been in use as a boom tug. Under her own power, she was brought to Leland by Louis Mosher and Morgan Cummings who, at that time, were employed by the Leland Blast Furnace Company.

With the launching of the *Leelanau*, there began a bitter feud between her master, Louis Mosher, and Captain John Harting, skipper of the *Tiger*, a craft that was already in service on Lake Leelanau (then Carp Lake), carrying passengers and baggage from Leland to Fouch, a distance of about eighteen miles. Traffic was met at the Fouch landing and brought to Traverse City by stage or train.

According to the tales, competition was bitter between the two skippers bidding for business. The fare for a round trip was originally $1.50. This, through the press of competition, was lowered to $1.00 and then to $.75. John Peters, who fired for four years on the *Leelanau*, expresses a belief that this price was one of the major factors in the final failure of the boat traffic.

Tragedy stalked the *Leelanau*. The *Ransom Brothers* had twice sunk in Buffalo waters. Brought to Leland, it was discovered she was too long for the river there and could not be turned around. She was eighty-seven feet overall. After the blast furnace company closed, she was left to sink her moorings.

Her boiler, installed in the new *Leelanau*, was the source of the next tragedy. This occurred just off Bingham Landing, according to those who remember, on a hot summer day in 1905, when Captain Mosher was steaming for the Fouch landing with a capacity load of gay excursionists. It was circus day in Traverse City. Perhaps the strain of a heavy load was too much for the old boiler or its age caused it to weaken, but there was a terrific roar. The vertical steam dome exploded. The irony of the accident was that John Harting, once captain of the *Tiger* and once rival of Mosher in lake traffic, was at the wheel. He had sold his ship and, longing for the wheel, made frequent trips on the *Leelanau*. Mosher usually permitted him to pilot the craft.

Mrs. Pasquel LaBonte was thrown overboard by the blast. Her body was not recovered for seven days. Scalding steam and water struck Harting in the back, causing fatal injuries. He died in the Traverse City Hospital.

The *Leelanau* remained for some time at Bingham Landing and was later sold to John VerSnyder. He installed a new engine and also a new boiler. The overall appearance of the craft was not altered, and she again began to ply the lake points. For a number of years he sailed the doughty little craft up and down the lake. Business was not always good, but there were usually a few passengers at Leland, or Provemont (Lake Leelanau), or Fountain Point, or one of the lumbering docks along the route.

Then ill health struck him. Late in 1929, he allowed the fire to die down under her boiler holding just enough steam to run her aground on the beach near the old VerSnyder home. He raked the coals out of her firepot and never set foot on her again. His illness grew worse; he was taken to Traverse City Hospital where he died.

Stories of the races between the *Tiger* and the *Leelanau* make good listening for the younger generation and they are not stories without foundation in fact.

The true pioneer spirit which rode with the two pilots has become a matter of record. When Captain Harting sold the *Tiger* to Bernie Pickard it was moved into Lake Michigan and used as a tug.

There was one other small craft that plied the Lake Leelanau waters for about three years during this era but was never considered serious competition. This was the *Sally*, owned by Morgan Cummings.

Anyone who wishes to see the remains of the old *Leelanau* will find the stark ribs and planks on the beach on the Wilburt Gauthier farm about three miles south of Lake Leelanau. The pilot house was, for some time, used as a playhouse by children. A considerable amount of timber from the *Leelanau* was built into the home of the Gauthiers. The boiler was taken to Traverse City and placed in use at the Grand Traverse Metal Casket Company factory.

Captain Dan Seavey

EVEN WHEN fact and fiction are separated and the glitter of retold tales is shadowed, Captain Daniel Seavey remains one of the most rugged and roistering characters ever to sail the Great Lakes. Captain Dan, if even a portion of the tales is to be accepted, was a hard-fighting, hard-drinking skipper who was never above a brawl in a bar-room or a bit of piracy to make a dollar. Master of his own schooner, the *Wanderer*, he was a familiar face in and around the Frankfort area in Benzie County.

Born at Portland, Maine, in 1865, he got the wanderlust at the age of thirteen or fourteen years. He sailed on commercial steamers and tramps for some time and did a hitch in the U. S. Navy. After that, he worked for the Department of Indian Affairs and sort of settled down on the east coast of Wisconsin. He operated a fish market in Milwaukee for a while and tried his hand at farming and at operating two saloons, which by some means he acquired.

The roaring days of the Alaskan gold rush lured him and he sold his wordly possessions and headed for the Yukon. He came home penniless, and the Great Lakes' ports were hungry for shipping facilities.

It was at this point in his colorful life that Dan Seavey began to gain the recognition which was to make him a legend up and down Lake Michigan. His first home port was Escanaba, and it was in that general area he became known as a robust man of the sea, ready to fight at the first excuse, yet kind and gentle when left alone or where children were involved.

Often repeated is a story out of Escanaba illustrating his liking for youngsters. A young lad, son of a well-to-do business man, liked to visit with the captain when he put into Escanaba. The lad's father felt that Dan was no fit company for his son and once caught him leaving the *Wanderer* at Merchant's dock.

Taking his son by the collar, he turned him over a firm knee and administered a sound thumping, receiving a promise that the lad would never see Captain Dan again. The punishment ended, the father and son turned towards home only to be halted by a heavy hand. Captain Seavey turned the father over his knee and administered painful punishment which he considered fitting to the crime.

Captain Dan fought in every port he visited if there was provocation. Always, after warping the *Wanderer* to the pier, the first stop was the nearest saloon, where he bought drinks for the house. One thing was certain, according to the old timers, every one had better drink with Captain Dan.

Dan's reputation as a bar-room brawler and all-around, rough-and-tumble fighter spread. From the Beavers to the southern tip of the Lake Michigan, he was respected for his ability to fight, any style.

Only once was he whipped. That was when some of the lads hired a professional boxer to pick a quarrel with him. The *Wanderer* was tied up at the dock at Escanaba and Dan was below deck. He heard footsteps above and investigated to find a scrawny little chap making himself at home.

The stranger taunted the captain to come ashore so he could trim him "down to my size." Captain Dan Seavey was never one to turn down an invitation to fight.

From the hands of the professional boxer, Seavey took a terrible beating. Staggering and bloody, he shook a big fist at the unmarked little rooster, "Come back here tomorrow, you tubercular little brat, and I'll give you another whipping," he screamed.

That was the way the story was told in the Kewaunee, Wisconsin, newspaper and, later, in the *Great Lakes Seafarer*.

Just how many of the stories told about Captain Dan are true will never be known. Many of them are. In the Frankfort area, there are those who remember seeing the captain stroll into a dimly lighted saloon carrying a bag full of skulls which he had unearthed somewhere in his wanderings. He delighted in slipping up behind a slightly bleary drinker, setting a grinning skull on the counter, giving with a scream and, then, roaring with laughter as the victim left by the nearest exit.

Somehow, Captain Seavey got appointed at one time to the post of

Deputy United States Marshal. One of his assignments was to track down a character who had been selling fire water to the Indians. In a saloon (where else?) in Naubinway, he caught up with the culprit, who told him that if he could drag him (the culprit) outside the building, he would go aboard Seavey's ship peacefully.

The two men fought, so the story goes, for several hours, stopping now and then for a drink. They wrecked the saloon. In a final, wild charge, Captain Dan finished the fight. He knocked his man to the floor and set a piano on his neck to keep him quiet. Thinking better, he took the piano off, but it was too late. The prisoner was dead. Captain Dan turned the body over for burial and went his way.

The story is told around Frankfort that Captain Dan would carry anything on his ship that he could roll or drag aboard, regardless of ownership. One cargo of lumber was being appropriated late one night at a Michigan port and, when the last board was stacked, he drove a "borrowed" team of oxen aboard, remarking if they didn't need them for unloading, they could eat them.

Another story still told in Frankfort is another classic of one of Dan's frequent fights. It was in the winter of 1904 and the bay was frozen over. Mitch Love, sporting a reputation as a real fighter, and Dan scratched a circle on the ice and went at it. There wasn't any real grudge. It was a matter of seeing who was the best man. They fought for two hours when Mitch could take no more and his friends carried him off the ice.

Another fight, which took place in Manistee, was "just for fun." Dan heard about someone in the Salt City who was extra good with his fists. The next time he was in Manistee, Dan called on the stranger. They met in a saloon, threw the customers out and wrecked the place before police stopped the brawl.

Thief, pirate, bar-room brawler, as you will, Captain Dan Seavey counted his friends by the thousands. He died penniless because he gave away countless thousands of dollars to children and to needy people. He had fists of iron and a heart of gold. Though he died a pauper in a convalescent home in Peshtigo, Wisconsin, in 1949, he lived to see himself become a legend on the lakes.

There's Gold in that Water

IT IS BELIEVED that the greatest single aggregation of wealth in the world lies at the bottom of the sea. There is no way to estimate the amount of money, treasure and marketable or merchantable material being drifted over by sand and silt beneath fathoms of water.

Countless thousands of dollars are represented in losses in the waters adjacent to the Grand Traverse region. Some of the rotted hulks are in reasonably shallow water while others lie in depths which make it difficult for even the most skillful divers to get at.

Within an area from Little Sable Point, south of Pentwater, to a north boundary near Eastport, including North and South Manitou Islands, at least two hundred ships have gone down in the past century and the approximate location of their sinking located and charted. The cargo of most of them has been determined.

Many of the craft which have been lost were in ballast. By that is meant the ship was running light, with no cargo other than bilge water and gear. Also, a majority of the sunken ships were lost in the days of the schooners. In fact, out of the two hundred, only forty-three were steamers or propellors. The remainder were schooners and, here and there, a bark, brig, or barge.

Only one ship has been lost in the waters immediately adjacent to Traverse City. It was the tug *Onward*, owned by Hannah, Lay and Company, which sank in ballast just north of Clinch Park in deep water. She sank in 1892 during a blow and is undoubtedly, today, beneath the shifting bottom of the bay. Her engine and gear would still be salvage, but the cost would be prohibitive.

Next in proximity to Traverse City would be the *John Thursby*, a sleek three-masted schooner which went down while heading a gale in 1867. She was loaded with fine china and she went down in deep water northwest of Ne-ah-ta-wanta Point in West Bay.

Another ship lost in Grand Traverse Bay was the *Pamilico*, a schooner which sank almost due east of Northport Point on the Eastport side of the bay. She was loaded with shingles.

The *Energy*, also a schooner carrying three masts, went down in a gale in 1854 while passing a point northeast of Old Mission Point and on the east side of the bay. She was loaded with a cargo of household goods of a wide variety.

A ship about which little is known was the *Brick*. She was a schooner loaded with a cargo of machinery. Of the kind of machinery she carried, or where she was bound, there is no record. The year when she sank, 1891, would indicate that she might have been carrying a sawmill for East Bay area operation.

Two ships lie on the bottom off Old Mission Point. Both of them were schooners. The *Metropolis*, carrying an unknown cargo, went on the rocks off the Point in 1886, and the *A. J. Rogers* broke in half when she went aground in 1898. She was loaded with iron. Both these craft are in reasonably shallow water.

In 1890, the *Ketcham*, in ballast, sank northeast of Lee's Point on the Leelanau side of West Bay. Prior to that, in 1872, the *Galena* went down during a storm and her grave is a short distance north of where the *Ketcham* sank. She had an unknown cargo.

Two more ships are known to lie on the bottom of Grand Traverse Bay. In 1860, the *Leander Choat* went down with a miscellaneous cargo. Her hull is on the bottom east and south of Northport beyond the harbor line. Off Northport Point, more officially known as Grand Traverse Point, lies the famous *Fanny Hazleton*. She sank in 1880 loaded with telephone poles.

One of the more romantic ships on the Great Lakes was the *Rising Sun*, owned and operated by the House of David cult at Benton Harbor. The cult owned High Island in the Beaver group and conducted an extensive farming program there. The *Rising Sun* was enroute from High Island to Benton Harbor in the fall of 1918. A storm came up from the lake when she was passing Good Harbor. In the emergency, the captain put in at the shelter but the storm grounded the craft, heavily loaded as it was with a year's accumulation of canned goods, grain and other crops, as well as a large number of passengers leaving High Island for the winter. The passengers were rescued when farmers in the Good Harbor area swam teams of horses to the doomed *Rising Sun* and took the passengers off to safety and shore. The entire cargo was lost.

In addition to the tug *Onward*, two more of the Hannah, Lay and Company fleet are on the bottom in Grand Traverse waters. The *J. Y. Scammon,* a brigantine, went down in 1854 off South Manitou Island. She was carrying a full miscellaneous cargo. All hands, including four women who were aboard at the time, were saved. She still lies in the same position where she sank. The *Queen of the Lakes*, a beautiful luxury craft designed for both passengers and trade, also sank off South Manitou.

While not lost in Traverse waters, other craft of the H. & L. fleet found watery graves in the Great Lakes or burned. The propellor *Manitou*, built in 1893, made three round trips each week between Chicago and Mackinac Island. She was sold in 1933 and renamed *Isle Royale*. She then did service between Chicago and Lake Superior ports but was badly damaged by fire while at dock in Manistee. Still later, she was converted to a barge and was finally cut up and scrapped.

The first steamer with the Hannah, Lay and Company was the *Sunnyside*. Built in 1864, she had four seasons of service in the Grand Traverse region. She was wrecked at dock at Pine River (Charlevoix) on November 14, 1867.

The *T. S. Faxton*, another passenger and freight steamer of the Company fleet, went into service in 1883 on the Traverse City, Petoskey, Mackinac daily line. On October 22, 1901, she burned at Marine City.

A schooner, the *Seamen*, with a capacity for 225,000 feet of lumber, built in Cleveland in 1848, did service for the Big Mill until 1905 when she was sold to M. O. Parker, Milwaukee. She went aground on Sleeping Bear in 1909. Prior to that, she had gone on South Manitou Island. South Manitou, offering a sheltering cove with relatively quiet water, was especially sought out during the days of the schooners, the barkentines and the brigs. For that reason, the waters around both North and South Manitou Islands are dotted with unmarked graves of sunken ships.

Many of the tragedies off these islands have been forgotten, although there are positive records of at least forty ships which have gone down in the waters between the north shore of North Island and Sleeping Bear Point. Stretch that distance to Frankfort and the total will be over sixty ships of various types.

What happens to the craft once they have settled to the bottom of the lake? Every deep sea diver and every modern skin diver would like to have all the answers.

According to Captain Arthur Frederickson, well known authority on Lake Michigan shipping, the bottom of the lake is never still. It seems to "breathe" and is constantly shifting with the motion of the water. Overnight, Captain Frederickson explains, the current of the bottom of the lake may completely cover or, by the same action, uncover an old ship.

"A diver may find an old schooner this week and mark it well. Next week, the entire hulk may be under several feet of sand and silt."

Frederickson, commenting on the possibility of salvage, explains that the cost of such operations is, in most cases, out of proportion to the value of any goods or material brought up, although such items as coal, quite a common cargo in the days of sailing ships, could be as good today as when it went down. Or pig iron, other than a loss from rust, would be logical salvage. A miscellaneous cargo, listed for a great number of craft, would be of doubtful value. Perhaps there would be a value from an historical viewpoint, but from the actual dollars-and-cents slant, it would be a poor investment.

Money, china, minerals of all sorts, machinery or materials manufactured from copper or brass, cast-iron items, cask goods in wooden containers and with wooden hoops, and of course, metal decking plates and so forth would be real money if they could be brought to the top without a large outlay of cash.

Just diving down in Lake Michigan and finding a wreck isn't going to turn it into cash. There is the matter of clearing away the sand and silt, cutting away barriers, hoisting salvage to a barge or other craft and finding a market. And, too, there are only a few days out of a season when a diver is able to work in deep water. It may look fine in the sky, but the weather beneath the gentle waves may be torn by murky and dark currents.

The fortunes are there, all right. There is no doubt about it. Each day more and more adventurers, some of them of good business background, are becoming interested in reclaiming lost cargo and, perhaps, in refloating an entire ship of another era.

FAMOUS FIRSTS IN THE GRAND TRAVERSE AREA

THE FIRST

white settlers in Grand Traverse County were Rev. Peter Dougherty and John Fleming, 1839.

frame building in the region was constructed at Old Mission by Rev. Dougherty, 1842.

church constructed in Grand Traverse County was in 1842 at Old Mission.

wedding in Grand Traverse County was that of Olive Dame to Ansel Salisbury of Wisconsin in the fall of 1842.

white child born in the region was Henry L. Miller, son of Mr. and Mrs. Lewis Miller, in 1846.

white settlers in Traverse City were Horace Boardman and Michael Gay in 1847.

residence in Traverse City was built in 1847 at the foot of Boardman Lake.

bridge constructed across the Boardman River was just south of Eighth Street and was built of poles, 1847.

white child born in Traverse City was Josephine Gay, daughter of the Michael Gays, on May 15, 1849.

mail service to the region was in June 1849, and consisted of two letters and a religious magazine, delivered by John Campbell.

postoffice was established in 1851 at Old Mission. W. R. Stone was postmaster; salary, nothing. Mail was kept in an empty raisin box nailed to the wall in the Stone kitchen.

steamer to enter Grand Traverse Bay was the *Michigan* on April 14, 1851.

mercantile establishment was the Hannah, Lay and Company, "dealers in everything."

steam sawmill was erected in 1852 by Hannah, Lay and Company.

white death recorded in Grand Traverse County occurred in 1852 and was a logging camp accident. No funeral services.

civic organization of record in Grand Traverse County was The Mutual Admiration Society.

school house in Grand Traverse County was in the 400 block East Front Street, 1853.

school teacher was Miss Helen R. Goodale, daughter of Dr. D. C. Goodale.

mail from the south was delivered by Indian Jake Tapasah in 1853.

marriage ceremony in Traverse City was that of James Lee and Ann Dakin in 1853.

Sabbath School in Traverse City started in 1853.

INDEX

Cook, Earl, 127
Cook, Frederick, 91
Coon, Eli, 160
Cooper, C. E., 118
Cooper, Charles, 119
Copeland, William, 129
Copley Township, 123
Core family, 94
Cornell, Elon, 127
Cornstalk, John, 7
Courturier family, 96
Cowgood, John, 87
Crain, L. W., Company, 60
Craker, Claude, 114
Craker, George, 114
Craker, Ruth, 114
Craker, W. A., 114
Craw Company, 138
Craw, Mark, 75, 148
Crawford County, 130
Creamery Corners, 65
Crescent (Steamer), 153
Croskoff, Fr. Clementine, 110
Cross Village, 7, 8
Croton, 36, 37
Crystal Lake, 78, 79, 80, 81
Crystal River, 106, 107
Culver, Waldo, 12, 13, 14
Cummings, Morgan, 163, 165
Curtis, D. C., 28
Custer, Gen. George A., 6
Cutler, Thomas, 32, 38

Dakin, Ann, 37, 174
Dame, Deacon, 92
Dame, Joseph, 92
Dame, Olive, 173
Darrow, Samuel Charles, 93, 94
Davis, Ray, 157
Davis, Steve, 134
Davis home, 135
Day, D. H., 105
Day, D. H., Lumber Company, 103

Day Forest Estate, 105
Dayhuff Lake, 122
Death Valley, 52
Decatur, 130
Degan, N. E., 86
DeGray, Frank, 76
Detroit, 22, 36, 39, 57
De Vries, Albert, 65
Dexter and Noble Company, 42, 130, 138–141, 143
Dezorme home, 6
"Dibbie," 51
Dill, William, 47
Donner family, 94
Dorsey, John, 91, 100, 103
Doty, Silas, 101
Dougherty, Rev. Peter, vii, 3, 112, 113, 114, 173
Douglas, Stephen, xi
Douglas Lumber Company, 55
Dover Township, 121
Duck Lake, 54, 55, 57
Dumbrille family, 105
DuPage County, Illinois, 2
Dupre, Charley, 6
Dutch Boy (Steamer), 155
Dyke, Aaron, 49
Dyke, William, 49

Eagletown, 7, 110-111
Earl, F. A., 104
Earl, F. A., Jewelry Store, 103
East Bay, 170
East Eighth Street, Traverse City, 22, 173
East Front Street, Traverse City, 32, 48, 174
East Jordan, 153
Eastport, 42, 169, 170
Eaton, A. W., 64, 65
Eaton, Charles, 67
Eaton and Stites Mill, 65, 66
Elk Lake, 145
Elk Rapids, 42, 91, 136, 137, 138, 143, 145

Elk Rapids Cement Plant, 136, 137
Elk Rapids Iron Company, 138
Ella Burrows (Steamer), 152
Ellis, Rev. Alvin, 132
Ellis Saloon, 75
Elm Flats, 148
Elmwood Avenue, Traverse City, 148
Emmerson, Charles, 46
Emory, Capt. J. U., 153
Energy (Schooner), 170
Engstrom, Gustav, 49
Engstrom, Pete, 49
Eric the Swede, 51
Erie, 28, 160
Escanaba, 166, 167
Europe, 36
Evers, Fr. Donulus, 110
Exchange, 74

Fairbanks family, 68
Fallass, S. S., 121, 122
Fannie Hazleton (Schooner), 170
Faxton, see T. S. Faxton
Ferguson, T. A., 118
Fernwood Hill, 7
Ferris, H. A., 73
Ferris, Mr., 159
Fife, William H., 69
Fife Lake, 69-72, 74, 132
Fife Lake Comet, 71
Fife Lake Eye, 71
Fife Lake Monitor, 71
Finucan, Capt. William, 154
Fisher, John E., 91, 103
Fisher, Mrs. John E., 104
Fisher, Pete, 60
Fisher, W. L., 93
Fisher family, 94
Fitzgerald, John, 31
Fitzgerald, Michael, 31
Fitzgerald, William, 31
Flarity, Mrs. Frank, 40, 41
Fleming, John, 173
Fond–du–Lac, 91, 92

Manuscript edited by Francis T. Majeske

Designed by William A. Bostick

Special reprint executed by

Harlo Printing Company

16721 Hamilton Avenue, Detroit, Michigan 48203